UNDERSTANDING THE PURPOSE AND POWER OF

PRAYER

EARTHLY LICENSE FOR HEAVENLY INTERFERENCE

DR. MYLES MUNROE

ᗯ
WHITAKER
HOUSE

UNDERSTANDING THE PURPOSE AND POWER OF PRAYER

Dr. Myles Munroe
Bahamas Faith Ministries International
P.O. Box N9583
Nassau, Bahamas
e-mail: bfmadmin@bfmmm.com
websites: www.bfmmm.com; www.bfmi.tv; www.mylesmunroe.tv

ISBN-13: 978-0-88368-442-9
ISBN-10: 0-88368-442-X
Printed in the United States of America
© 2002 by Dr. Myles Munroe

Whitaker House
1030 Hunt Valley Circle
New Kensington, PA 15068
www.whitakerhouse.com

Library of Congress Cataloging-in-Publication Data
Munroe, Myles.
Understanding the purpose and power of prayer / by Myles Munroe.
  p.   cm.
ISBN 0-88368-442-X (pbk. : alk. paper)
1. Prayer.   I. Title.
BV215 .M83 2002
248.3'2—dc21
               2002005024

9 10 11 12 13 14 15 16 17 ᴜᴊ 15 14 13 12 11 10 09 08 07

Dedication

To my late mother, Princess Louise Munroe, who taught me the value and power of prayer, and through whose prayers all of her children have come to know for themselves the virtue of this divine art.

To my late mother-in-law, "Madam" Emily Lockhart, who was a constant personal prayer covering over the years. I know you continue to join Jesus in prayer for us still. Thanks for praying for "every mother's child." We love you always.

To my personal intercessors, Gloria Seymour, Alma Trotman, Ingrid Johnson, Pat Butler, Mirthlyn Jones, Beverly Lockhart, and the many others who have undergirded me over the years. I love you all.

To every intercessor who labors daily in the Spirit to bring God's will on earth through consistent prayers.

To all who desire to understand and experience a dynamic prayer life and a deeper walk with their Creator.

To the Lord Jesus, in whose name all our petitions are made and heard and answered.

Acknowledgments

Nothing in life is ever successful without the corporate effort of many gifted people who are willing to network and submit their talent, experience, and passion for a common goal. We are the sum total of all the people we have met and learned from. This work is a product of countless individuals whose thoughts, ideas, perspectives, and work have given me the exposure to the knowledge I have placed in this book.

I wish to thank my beautiful wife, Ruth, and our children, Charisa and Chairo (Myles, Jr.), for their patience and understanding during my endless travels and late nights writing. My achievements are yours, also.

To Lois Puglisi, my excellent editor and guide in developing this manuscript—you are an author's dream and a gift to the many who will read this work. Thank you for pursuing me to get this done.

To Dr. Lucille Richardson, for her deep commitment and dedication to excellence and loyalty to my reputation—I cherish your life and the part it plays in mine.

Contents

Preface

There is nothing more common among men, no human activity more universal, yet none more mysterious and misunderstood, than prayer. Since the dawn of time and the advent of recorded history, the religious expression of prayer has been found in every culture, civilization, and era. Primitive tribes on every continent to complex civilizations around the world have been known to practice this ancient art called prayer to some god or deity.

Psychologists and behavioral scientists have long studied the effects of prayer on human development and socialization. Some studies have even attempted to validate and document the effectiveness of prayers on the individual practicing the art.

There is no shortage of skeptics and antagonists who frown on those who believe that such human superstition and fanatical religious tradition could impact human experience or the course of life on earth. The atheist does not even acknowledge that there is someone out there listening. To these cynics, prayer is simply a human invention designed as an outlet for the fears, frustration, and anxiety of man—nothing more than a psychological experience that eases the mind and helps to cope with life's challenges.

Yet the question must be answered, why do men pray? Hundreds of millions of people around the world participate in this ritual every day in every language, race, and culture. Why do people of every religion pray? All the major religions require their adherents to practice regular daily prayers. Why? Why is the human spirit naturally drawn to seek solace and comfort in the unseen and unknown? Is there a mystery that man still does not comprehend? Why should and—why do we—pray?

These questions and many more inspired me to write this book. I, too, had my questions and doubts regarding prayer. Many individuals who practice this religious activity are afraid to ask questions about it openly. Some practice it without believing it. To many, it is only a ritual with no reality.

Some have been discouraged because they have had the feeling that prayer is a fruitless ritual with no evidence of tangible results. Many more have just simply quit the practice and avoided any opportunity to participate in it.

If we wish to be honest, more among us than not are suffering from a silent disillusionment with our experience of this ritual called prayer. We have asked ourselves: Does it really work? Is someone listening? Does it make a difference? Can it truly change circumstances?

While prayer is so common, it is also mysterious and misunderstood. It seems as if it is the most commonly practiced unknown on planet earth. Scores of books have been written on the subject in every generation. Conferences and seminars are held everywhere to explore the mysteries of this ancient art called prayer.

Despite all the questions, confusion, and uncertainty surrounding prayer, though, it is still the greatest common denominator among all the great biblical characters and thousands of believers throughout history. Moses practiced it. Abraham practiced it. King David, Solomon, Esther, Deborah, Daniel, Joseph, all the prophets—and, of course, Jesus Christ Himself—had dynamic and profound commitments to lives of prayer. Their records show the direct impact of their prayers on their lives and on the circumstances and situations they faced. The evidence affirms that one thing is sure: No matter what you may think about prayer, somehow it works.

The real question is not one of whether prayer is valid or effective, but rather, do we understand the art and know how it works? It is this challenge that we will embrace in this work as we explore the principles and precepts established by the Creator regarding prayer and discover the keys to unlocking the purpose and power of this common, yet uncommon, divine art. Let us begin by taking a journey through the land of doubt, shedding the skepticism, and activating the most awesome power every human being possesses: the power to influence earth from heaven through prayer.

Introduction

The President of the United States does it, the Prime Minister of Israel does it, the Chairman of the Palestinian People does it, and the Queen of England does it.

Jews do it, Muslims do it, Hindus do it, Buddhists do it, pagans do it, heathens do it, Christians do it, everyone does it. Few are sure it works, and even less believe it is necessary. What is it?

Prayer!

Prayer could be designated as the first global product of religion. No matter how diverse the religions of the world may be, one common ritual and practice that they all embrace is prayer. Prayer is religion's neutralizer.

Yet prayer is still the most elusive and misunderstood practice of religious adherents ever. To understand prayer is the desire of every man's heart; even the pagan longs to connect with the divine and find comfort, access, and results. Understanding it, though, takes some work.

****

It was the first day after he had made a personal commitment to follow the Christian faith and learn the way of Jesus Christ. Thomas was shocked to see just a handful of people in the large building that just the day before was overflowing with dedicated worshippers.

"Where is everyone?" Thomas asked as his eyes surveyed the sea of empty chairs in the auditorium.

"I'm not sure," answered Cory, "but this is the way it is at every Monday night prayer meeting.

"But yesterday there were thousands here for corporate worship," Thomas said, with a look of bewilderment, "Don't they pray? I thought all Christians prayed. Why are they not here? Why don't they come to prayer meeting like they attend the regular worship service?"

Cory suddenly knew he could not answer Thomas's mental questions well enough to satisfy his passion for truth, so he decided to explain from his perspective why the prayer meeting in almost every church in the city was the smallest and least attended service.

"I believe it is because many of them have not had a good experience with this prayer thing," Cory said. "All the hype and promises attached to it do not seem to work for most of them, so they avoid the negative experience. Why have you come?"

"I guess I came because I believe it works," Thomas answered, "but I don't know why or how. So to be sure, I want to have it covered."

****

Similar situations are repeated all over the world in a multitude of religious settings. The question is, why? Why do so many avoid prayer? Perhaps it is because the human spirit hates failure and disappointments. It's like putting money into a soda machine that doesn't give a can of pop in return. You stand in front of it, becoming increasingly frustrated, until you finally kick it and walk away. But you also never attempt to use it again. This is how many people feel about prayer. They have put in too many prayer coins and have received too few satisfying answers.

Why doesn't prayer seem to work? To answer this question, we must first understand the source, principles, origin, and purpose of prayer. What is prayer? Why is prayer necessary? How should we pray? Why pray to God in the name of Jesus? Why is prayer not always answered the way we expect? When should we stop praying? What role does faith have in the prayer process? Do we have to "qualify" to pray? If God is sovereign and can do whatever He wishes, then why pray? Does prayer affect or change destiny?

The questions go on and on, and I know you can probably add many more to the list. However, these questions only indicate the tremendous confusion and misconceptions surrounding prayer.

So, how are we to understand prayer? I remember the many times I attended prayer meetings and, even while I was praying, wondered whether it was worth it or if prayer really worked at all. There were times when I only went through the motions, even as a Christian leader, with no belief in the very act of prayer I was participating in.

I am certain that my struggles with the prayer issue are not unique to me. I have spoken with countless individuals who also have struggled with it. Some still struggle to understand its practice and to believe in its validity.

It was not until I understood the principle of purpose and faithfulness that I began to grasp the nature, philosophy, and foundation of the concept of prayer and experience the power and positive results of prayer in my own life.

THE FOUNDATION OF PRAYER

To understand the principle of prayer, it is necessary to understand the mind and purpose of the Creator Himself. Prayer is a result of God's established authority structure between heaven and earth, as well as a product of His faithfulness to His Word. Prayer is as simple as respecting God's authority. This is because prayer was born out of God's arrangements for man's assignment on earth; it happened when the Creator spoke two words during the creation process: *"let them."* These words are recorded in the first chapter of the first book of the Bible:

> Then God said, *"Let us make man in our image, in our likeness, and **let them** rule over the fish of the sea and the birds of the air, over the livestock, over all the earth, and over all the creatures that move along the ground."* (Gen. 1:26–27, emphasis added)

These words are critical in understanding the principle of prayer, since they define the relationship the Creator intended and desired with man and the planet earth.

The Creator's mandate for man to dominate the earth was established in the declaration, but the parameters of that dominion were established with the words, *"Let them."*

By these words, the Creator defined the boundaries of His right to legally influence and interfere in the earth realm. This is based on the principle of God's integrity and

His commitment to His Word. Why is this so important? Because of these four principles:

- God's purpose is more important than our plans.
- God has placed His Word above even Himself.
- God will never violate or break His word.
- God's holiness is the foundation of His integrity and faithfulness.

These principles are essential to an understanding of the nature and purpose of prayer. It is these precepts that make prayer necessary.

The first principle establishes the truth that the Creator's commitment to His original intent for creation is a priority for Him and motivates and regulates all His actions. In essence, everything He does is driven by His purposed desire, which never changes. In fact, His declaration is clear when He states, *"Many are the plans in a man's heart, but it is the LORD's purpose that prevails"* (Prov. 19:21–22). Again, He declares,

> *I make known the end from the beginning, from ancient times, what is still to come. I say: My purpose will stand, and I will do all that I please."*
> (Isa. 46:10–11)

> *So is my word that goes out from my mouth: It will not return to me empty, but will accomplish what I desire and achieve the purpose for which I sent it.*
> (Isa. 55:11–12)

> *In Him we were also chosen, having been predestined according to the plan of Him who works out everything in conformity with the purpose of his will.*
> (Eph. 1:11)

> *Because God wanted to make the unchanging nature of his purpose very clear to the heirs of what was promised, he confirmed it with an oath.* (Heb. 6:17)

Finally, His commitment to His purpose is expressed in these words:

Introduction

I tell you the truth, until heaven and earth disappear, not the smallest letter, not the least stroke of a pen, will by any means disappear from the Law until everything is accomplished. (Matt. 5:18–19)

These statements reveal God's eternal, uncompromising commitment to His purpose and plans. His purpose is His will and intent, which He Himself will fulfill. However, it is essential to know that His commitment to fulfill His purpose will never be at the expense of violating His spoken or written word.

It is this commitment to His Word that is the basis of the prayer principle. The Word of God is not just the law for man, for it is also called "the Law of God." This implies that every word God speaks is also a law to Himself. He will subject Himself to His promises and decrees because of His integrity.

In the book of Psalms, we find these words:

Your word, O Lord, is eternal; it stands firm in the heavens. Your faithfulness continues through all generations. (Ps. 119:89–90)

I will bow down toward your holy temple and will praise your name for your love and your faithfulness, for you have exalted above all things your name and your word. (Ps. 138:2)

The fact that He places His Word above all things, including His name, is an important principle because one of the Hebrew concepts for name is "the being" itself. Therefore, in application, God places His Word above Himself, submitting Himself to the dictates of His own Word.

In effect, whenever God speaks, He Himself is willfully obligated to obey His own Word. Therefore, any law of God is a law to God. He is faithful to His Word at all costs. This being understood, we can appreciate the implications and impact of these initial words spoken by the Creator at man's creation: *"Let them have dominion over...the earth"* (Gen. 1:26).

Please note that He did not say, "Let us," but rather, *"Let them."* With this statement, God created seven primary laws:

- The legal authority to dominate earth was given to mankind only.
- God did not include Himself in the legal authority structure over the earth.
- Man became the legal steward of the earth domain.
- Man is a spirit with a physical body; therefore, only spirits with physical bodies can legally function in the earth realm.
- Any spirit without a body is illegal on earth.
- Any influence or interference from the supernatural realm on earth is only legal through mankind.
- God Himself, who is a Spirit without a physical body, made Himself subject to this law.

The following are the results of these laws, which were established by God Himself:

- The legal authority on earth is in the hands of humankind.
- The Creator, because of His integrity, will not violate the law of His Word.
- Nothing will happen in the earth realm without the active or passive permission of man, who is its legal authority.
- The Creator and the heavenly beings cannot interfere in the earth realm without the cooperation or permission of mankind.
- God must obtain the agreement and cooperation of a person for whatever He desires to do in the earth.

These principles are critical for understanding the nature, power, and purpose of prayer. It is from these precepts that we get our definition of prayer. In this work, the following will comprise the definition of prayer, which will become clearer as we progress together in exploring the wonders of this art.

WHAT IS PRAYER?

- Prayer is man giving God the legal right and permission to interfere in earth's affairs.

Introduction

- Prayer is man giving heaven earthly license to influence earth.
- Prayer is a terrestrial license for celestial interference.
- Prayer is man exercising his legal authority on earth to invoke heaven's influence on the planet.

These definitive aspects of prayer may be a little shocking to many, but a closer study will better explain many statements made in Scripture as they relate to heavenly activities on earth. Let's take a look at a few:

If my people, who are called by my name, will humble themselves and pray and seek my face and turn from their wicked ways, then will I hear from heaven and will forgive their sin and will heal their land.
(2 Chron. 7:14)

Then Jesus told his disciples a parable to show them that they should always pray and not give up.
(Luke 18:1–2)

And pray in the Spirit on all occasions with all kinds of prayers and requests. With this in mind, be alert and always keep on praying for all the saints.
(Eph. 6:17–18)

Be joyful always; pray continually without ceasing; give thanks in all circumstances, for this is God's will for you in Christ Jesus. (1 Thess. 5:16–19)

I will give you the keys of the kingdom of heaven; whatever you bind on earth will be bound in heaven, and whatever you loose on earth will be loosed in heaven. (Matt. 16:19–20)

I tell you the truth, whatever you bind on earth will be bound in heaven, and whatever you loose on earth will be loosed in heaven. Again, I tell you that if two of you on earth agree about anything you ask for, it will be done for you by my Father in heaven. For where two or three come together in my name, there am I with them. (Matt. 18:18–20)

These Scriptures give mankind the authority and prerogative to determine what happens on earth. In fact, a careful biblical study of God's dealings with mankind and the earth reveals that He did nothing on earth without the cooperation of a person.

Every action taken by God in the earth realm required the involvement of a human being. To rescue humanity in the Flood, He needed Noah. For the creation of a nation, He needed Abraham. To lead the nation of Israel, He needed Moses. To bring back Israel from captivity, He needed Daniel. To defeat Jericho, He needed Joshua. For the preservation of the Hebrews, He needed Esther. For the salvation of mankind, *He needed to become a man.*

As John Wesley once said, "God does nothing but in answer to prayer."[*]

Prayer is therefore not an option for mankind but a necessity. If we don't pray, heaven cannot interfere in earth's affairs. It is imperative that we take responsibility for the earth and determine what happens here by our prayer lives.

I invite you to discover your power, authority, and rights in the earth and to position yourself to become a faith channel for heavenly influence in earth's affairs. Heaven depends on you, and earth needs you. Without you, heaven will not—and without heaven, earth cannot.

Remember Jesus' great prayer request when He was asked by His disciples how man should pray: *"This, then, is how you should pray: Our Father in heaven, hallowed be your name, your kingdom come, your will be done on earth as it is in heaven"* (Matt. 6:9–11).

Heaven needs you to give it license to impact earth. You can make a difference and change the course of history if you will just understand the purpose and power of prayer. Join me on this adventure into the heart of prayer and watch your power of attorney explode into a dynamic life of purposeful petition for heavenly impact on earth.

---

[*] Quoted in E. M. Bounds, *Power through Prayer,* Chapter 11, "The Example of the Apostles," published by Whitaker House.

Part I

The Purpose and Priority of Prayer

Chapter One

Does Prayer Really Work?

Prayer is one of the most misunderstood arts of the human experience—yet it is meant to be one of the most exciting aspects of a life of faith.

Prayer is a lonely experience for many of us. Although we have been taught that it is important to pray, we have been so disappointed and frustrated that our prayers haven't been answered, we've almost given up on it. We may pray when we are scared or sick, but it's not a regular practice in our lives. Outwardly, we agree that prayer is worthwhile, but secretly we wonder:

Does God really hear me when I pray?

Why does it seem as if my prayers just hit the ceiling and bounce back at me?

Is God mad at me? Is that why He doesn't answer me?

Why is prayer so boring and fruitless for me?

Shouldn't I expect my prayers to be answered?

Unanswered prayer is a major obstacle that stands in the way of a life of true faith. Certain people have lost their faith altogether because of unanswered prayer. Some have turned to philosophy, metaphysics, or cults to find answers to life's questions and problems. Others have turned to horoscopes, psychic hotlines, and witchcraft. Still others have rejected the spiritual realm completely and now focus on purely materialistic things.

Confusion about prayer also affects those who are committed Christians. The greatest difficulty in most believers' experience is their prayer lives. Even though they believe prayer is a foundational element of the Christian life, they shy away from it because they don't really think it will make a difference. They don't pray because it hasn't seemed to work for them in the past, and they don't like failure. Some have been tempted to delve into ungodly activities because they were weary of not having their prayers answered.

The greatest difficulty in most believers' experience is their prayer lives.

For many who do pray, the practice of prayer is merely a religious exercise, one that isn't concerned with obtaining results. Some believers have come to the conclusion—consciously or subconsciously—that prayer isn't very important to everyday life, that it doesn't apply to the real world. They look primarily to themselves or other people to meet their needs.

We can measure how much the average Christian really believes in the effectiveness of prayer by the small number of people who attend prayer meetings in our churches. Prayer is not a priority for us. Other activities seem more exciting and fruitful. We don't mind attending Bible studies, participating in ministry outreaches, serving on church committees, or being involved in other such activities, but we avoid prayer—both individually and corporately—because we don't understand it.

Even believers who pray regularly with conviction and obtain some results have doubts about certain aspects of prayer: what they are supposed to ask for, how long they should continue praying for something, and similar questions concerning the nature of prayer. In general, there is a lack of teaching, interest, and understanding about prayer in the church.

Our disappointing experiences with prayer have caused us to question, "Will God's Word do what it says it will do?" We're not sure anymore. We still read the Bible and listen to preaching and teaching from the Word of God, and we know that the Word is supposed to work, but we haven't had many successful experiences with the fulfillment of

God's Word in our lives beyond our initial experience of salvation.

CONSEQUENCES OF UNANSWERED PRAYER

Frustration and confusion over unanswered prayer are understandable. We expect things to work if God said they are supposed to work. Therefore, when our prayers seem to go unanswered, what effect does this have on us? The spiritual and emotional pain can be deep and devastating. It can lead to sorrow, despair, bitterness, and rebellion. It can undermine the foundation of our faith and lead to these results:

The spiritual and emotional pain of unanswered prayer can be deep and devastating.

1. *We feel abandoned and isolated from God, imagining that He doesn't care about our problems.* As a result, we begin to doubt His love for us. We start to view Him as someone who is against us—or at least indifferent to us—instead of as a loving heavenly Father who gives good gifts to His children.
2. *We question God's character and integrity.* We may wonder, "Does God promise to answer my prayers or doesn't He? Can I rely on Him to fulfill His Word?" In this way, we begin to distrust Him, eroding our basis for belief and causing our relationship with Him to suffer.
3. *We feel as if our lives are very unsettled and unstable.* We may ask, "Can I really depend on God, or is prayer a hit-or-miss proposition? What can I really count on in regard to prayer?" Therefore, we begin to rely on ourselves, or on other people, groups, or beliefs, instead of appropriating the power and promises of God to meet our needs.
4. *We come to premature conclusions about ourselves and our prayers.* For example, when we try to make sense of why our prayers aren't working, we may assume, "My prayers aren't answered because I don't have enough faith." Therefore, we don't come to understand the various principles and truths concerning prayer that God has given us in His Word for our benefit.

5. *We doubt our calling as God's intercessors.* We begin to think, "Answered prayer must be only for an elite group of 'super-spiritual' Christians." In this way, we abandon a major purpose of God for our lives.

When we experience these consequences of unanswered prayer, we are tempted to ask the question posed in Job 21:15: *"What would we gain by praying to him?"* Yet the question really is: What are we *losing* by not praying to Him?

Many Christians today are experiencing powerlessness, lack of direction, little victory over sin, poor spiritual progress, a weak witness, unfruitful ministry, poverty, and other similar problems. Is there any connection between underdeveloped, defeated, or directionless lives and confusion over prayer? In my experience, a strong connection often exists. A great many believers don't have successful prayer lives—and successful lives in general—because they simply don't know how or why to pray. Other Christians know some of the principles of prayer but are not fulfilling their full potential as intercessors because they don't understand certain key aspects of prayer.

Prayer is not just an activity, a ritual, or an obligation. It is communion and communication that touches God's heart.

THE MISUNDERSTOOD ART OF PRAYER

I am convinced that prayer is one of the most misunderstood arts of the human experience. Prayer is not just an activity, a ritual, or an obligation. Nor is it begging God to do what we want Him to do. It is communion and communication with God that touches His heart. When you understand the principles of the art of prayer, you will begin to communicate with God with power, grace, and confidence.

Prayer is meant to be one of the most exciting aspects of a life of faith. It has the power to transform lives, change circumstances, give peace and perseverance in the midst of trial, alter the course of nations, and win the world for Christ.

The power of prayer is the inheritance of the believer. My goal for this book is to demystify prayer so that believers can make use of what is rightfully theirs in Christ. My approach is very practical. It is based on the clear teaching of the Word of God and over thirty years of personal experience in which I have, by God's grace, learned how to pray and receive answers to my prayers. I know what it means to struggle with prayer.

Therefore, I can understand the pain of unanswered prayer that many Christians are experiencing—that you may be experiencing right now. Yet because I have learned and tested the truths of prayer, I also know the joy of its fulfillment. I've come to recognize many of the obstacles that prevent prayer from being answered, as well as many of the principles of effective prayer. These principles are not obscure. They are readily available for you to begin practicing today.

THE PATHWAY TO PRAYER

If we are to clear away the fog of confusion over prayer so that we may see its features more clearly, we must start by understanding the following truths:

First, we must realize that when prayer does not bring results, it is an indication that something is wrong. God instituted prayer, and throughout the Old and New Testaments, there are numerous examples of prayers offered and answered. When prayer isn't answered, the Word of God generally provides an indication of why it was not answered, gives insight into the kind of prayers God responds to, and points out what can inhibit our prayers.

This is not to say that the answers to our prayers will always be immediately manifested. However, it does mean that every prayer based on the Word of God and offered in faith by a person who is in right relationship with God *is answered*—and that it is only a matter of time before that answer is evidenced. God answers as soon as we ask, and He reveals those answers in His timing. That is why Jesus told His disciples *"that they should always pray and not give up"* (Luke 18:1).

Second, God is faithful to answer prayer. Our understanding of prayer has become so distorted that we have developed a definition for the word that is the exact opposite of its true meaning. When we say something has no chance, or only a slight chance, of happening, we say, "It hasn't got a prayer." Yet Jesus gives us the assurance that God does hear and answer our prayers. He said, *"Therefore I tell you, whatever you ask for in prayer, believe that you* **have received** *it, and it will be yours"* (Mark 11:24, emphasis added). The answer is so sure that we are instructed to believe it has already happened.

Third, God's will and Word **do** *work when they are understood and put into practice.* Whether you think so right now or not, prayer *does* work. However, it first needs to be understood. We must learn how to pray in a way that embodies the truths and principles of prayer that God has given us in His Word. The purpose of this book is to clearly set forth these truths and principles. True prayer will do the following:

- build intimacy with God
- bring honor to His nature and character
- cause respect for His integrity
- enable belief in His Word
- cause a trust in His love
- affirm His purposes and will
- appropriate His promises

We must pray in a way that embodies the principles God has given us in His Word.

God is loving and gracious. He knows we have a limited understanding of Himself and His ways, and that we struggle with our fallen nature. That is why He will at times answer our prayers even when they are weak and full of doubt. However, as a loving Father, He wants us to grow and mature. He doesn't want to leave us in our weakness and uncertainty. He wants us to enter into His purposes, because that is where we can truly be children of our heavenly Father, work together with Him, and live the abundant life Christ came to give us (John 10:10). Therefore, at times, He will withhold answers to prayer so we will seek Him and the principles of prayer that are essential for praying according to His will and for appropriating His promises and power.

Because of the nature of prayer and because God wants us to grow in our faith, praying without understanding or applying the principles of prayer is usually ineffective. I would even say it is a waste of time. It brings frustration and causes believers to remain in the middle of problems and circumstances that can be overcome through prayer—leaving them unable to fulfill their calling as God's priests and ambassadors in the world. Prayer is meant to be answered—or else God would not ask us to pray. He isn't interested in wasting your time and efforts. He is too practical for that. He is interested in results, not just *"many words"* (Matt. 6:7) spoken in prayer. Jesus' approach to prayer was also very practical. He didn't pray without expecting to be heard. At one point He said, *"Father, I thank you that you have heard me. I knew that you **always** hear me"* (John 11:41–42, emphasis added). We need to know how to approach God and to learn the kind of prayers God responds to. We need to pray as Jesus prayed.

REMOVING THE OBSTACLE OF UNANSWERED PRAYER

Through the truths and principles outlined in this book, you can begin today to change your outlook on God, yourself, and prayer. You can have an effective prayer life that will overflow into all other areas of your life. It is God's desire that you experience intimacy with Him and spiritual strength to fulfill His purposes. The principles you discover will help you to clear away the obstacle of unanswered prayer that has been holding you back from fulfilling your purpose so you can enter into a new dimension of faith, deep love for God, and power for service.

LET'S PRAY TOGETHER

Heavenly Father,

You have said, *"Call to me and I will answer you and tell you great and unsearchable things you do not know"* (Jer. 33:3). On the basis of this promise, we call to You and ask You to show us great and unsearchable truths about prayer that You have set forth in Your Word. Forgive us for leaning on our own understanding when it comes to prayer. Heal us from the spiritual and emotional effects that unanswered prayer have worked in us. Give us open minds and hearts to hear Your Word and to allow the Holy Spirit to teach us Your purposes and truth. We pray this in the name of Jesus, our Wisdom and our Strength. Amen.

PUTTING PRAYER INTO PRACTICE

As we learn about prayer, our greatest temptation will be to acquire knowledge about prayer without putting it into practice. That is why, at the end of each chapter, there will be a section called "Putting Prayer into Practice." I encourage you to think about and respond to the questions and action steps presented in these sections. May God bless you as you discover the purpose and power of prayer.

Ask yourself—

- How often do I pray?
- Is prayer a mystery to me? Are there aspects of prayer that are confusing or unclear to me?
- Have I experienced unanswered prayer? How has that made me feel about prayer, about God, and about myself?
- Am I experiencing powerlessness, lack of direction, little victory over sin, poor spiritual progress, a weak witness, unfruitful ministry, poverty, or other similar problems?
- How would answered prayer make a difference in my life?

Principles

1. Unanswered prayer is a major obstacle that stands in the way of a life of true faith.

2. Unanswered prayer can lead to these results:
   - We feel abandoned and isolated from God, imagining that He doesn't care about our problems and doubting His love.
   - We question God's character and integrity, and we begin to distrust Him.
   - We feel as if our lives are very unsettled and unstable; therefore, we begin to rely on ourselves, or on other people, groups, or beliefs, instead of God.
   - We come to premature conclusions about ourselves and our prayers, and so we don't learn the principles and truths of prayer that God has given in His Word.
   - We doubt our calling as God's intercessors, so that we abandon a major purpose of God for our lives.

3. A great many believers don't have successful prayer lives—and successful lives in general—because they simply don't know how or why to pray.

4. Some Christians know certain principles of prayer, but are not fulfilling their full potential as intercessors because they don't understand key aspects of prayer.

5. The power of prayer is the inheritance of the believer.

6. To understand prayer, we need to recognize the following:
   - Prayer activity that does not bring results is an indication that something is wrong.
   - God is faithful to answer prayer.
   - God's will and Word *do* work when they are understood and put into practice.

7. True prayer builds intimacy with God, honors His nature and character, respects His integrity, believes His Word, trusts in His love, affirms His purposes and will, and appropriates His promises.

8. Praying without understanding and applying the truths and principles of prayer is ineffective.

9. Prayer is meant to be answered—or God would not ask us to pray. Jesus didn't pray without expecting to be heard.

Chapter Two

The Genesis of Prayer

Prayer is mankind exercising dominion on the earth by giving God the freedom to intervene in earth's affairs.

W hen we pray but don't receive answers to our prayers, we may wonder: "What is the purpose of prayer? Doesn't God do whatever He wants to do, anyway? Why should we have to pray when God already—

- knows everything
- controls everything
- predetermines everything
- does not change?"

These are valid questions. To answer them, we first need to understand essential truths about God's nature and His purposes for mankind that lead to the necessity of prayer. The biblical account of the creation of humanity reveals these truths.

To begin with, God does everything for a reason, because He is a God of purpose. His actions are not arbitrary. *"The LORD Almighty has sworn, 'Surely, as I have planned, so it will be, and as I have purposed, so it will stand'"* (Isa. 14:24). *"The plans of the LORD stand firm forever, the purposes of his heart through all generations"* (Ps. 33:11). *"Many are the plans in a man's heart, but it is the Lord's purpose that prevails"* (Prov. 19:21). God is a God of purpose, and everything He has created in this world, including men and women, has been created to fulfill His purposes. Therefore, when God said, *"Let us make man in our image, in our likeness"* (Gen. 1:26), what does this statement reveal about His purposes for humanity and the reason for prayer?

HUMANITY WAS CREATED TO REFLECT GOD'S NATURE AND TO HAVE FELLOWSHIP WITH HIM

First, God created humanity to reflect His character and personality. We were created to be like Him, having His *"image"* and *"likeness"* (Gen. 1:26). This means we were created to have His nature and moral character. That was meant to be the essence of our being. The personal reason God created mankind was to establish a relationship of mutual love with humanity. God created mankind in His own image so love could be freely given and received between Creator and created. The only reason man can have fellowship with God is that God made man out of His own essence. He made man to be spirit, just as He is Spirit. *"God is spirit, and his worshipers must worship in spirit and in truth"* (John 4:24).

> **Humanity cannot reveal God's image and likeness apart from a relationship with Him.**

Although God is the Creator, He has always emphasized that He is man's Father. It wasn't His desire to be primarily thought of as an awesome God or a *"consuming fire"* (Deut. 4:24). God wants us to approach Him as a child would a loving father: *"Is he not your Father, your Creator, who made you and formed you?"* (Deut. 32:6). *"As a father has compassion on his children, so the LORD has compassion on those who fear him"* (Ps. 103:13).

Man was created out of the essence of God, yet is always dependent on God as his Source. As human beings, we are not self-sufficient, even though we would like to think we are. We cannot reveal God's image and likeness apart from a relationship with Him. We were intended to reflect God's nature in the context of being continually connected to Him in fellowship. First John 4:16 says, *"Whoever lives in love lives in God, and God in him."* No human being is going to be truly satisfied with life until he or she loves God. God must have the primary place in our lives because we were designed to find fulfillment and ultimate meaning in Him.

HUMANITY WAS CREATED TO HAVE DOMINION

Second, God created humanity to carry out His purposes in the earth. This is mankind's primary vocation. When God created man in His image, He gave him a free will. In this way, man was given the ability to plan and make decisions, and then to take action to fulfill those plans, just as God did in creating the world. Man was meant to carry out God's purposes for the earth using his own will and initiative. He was to reflect the God who plans in advance and carries out His plans through creative acts.

How was humanity to fulfill this vocation?

> Then God said, "Let us make man in our image, in our likeness, and let them rule ["have dominion" NKJV] over the fish of the sea and the birds of the air, over the livestock, over all the earth, and over all the creatures that move along the ground." So God created man in his own image, in the image of God he created him; male and female he created them. God blessed them and said to them, "Be fruitful and increase in number; fill the earth and subdue it. Rule over the fish of the sea and the birds of the air and over every living creature that moves on the ground."
>
> (Gen. 1:26–28)

God said, "Let us make man in our image, in our likeness, and **let them rule** ["have dominion" NKJV]" (Gen. 1:26, emphasis added). Amazingly, man was created not only to have a relationship with God, but also to share God's authority. "You made him ruler over the works of your hands; you put everything under his feet" (Ps. 8:6). "The highest heavens belong to the LORD, but the earth he has given to man" (Ps. 115:16).

How did God enable man to rule on earth? We know that He first created mankind out of His own essence, which is *spirit*. Yet since mankind needed to be able to rule in the *physical* realm of earth, God then gave humanity physical bodies manifested in two genders—male and female. This is why the Bible refers to the creation of man in both singular and plural terms: "So God created man in his *own image, in the image of God he created him; male and female he created them"* (Gen. 1:27). The word *"man"* in the twenty-sixth and twenty-seventh verses of Genesis 1 refers to the *species* that God made, the spirit-being called "man," which includes both male and female. This means that the purpose of dominion was given to both men and women.[*]

The account of the creation of mankind shows us that God never desired or intended to rule the earth by Himself. Why? It is because *"God is love"* (1 John 4:8, 16), and love doesn't think in those terms. A selfish person wants all the glory, all the credit, all the power, all the authority, all the rights, and all the privileges. But a person of love wants others to share in what he has. It is crucial for us to understand that the *relationship of love* that God established with mankind is not separate from the *purpose* God has for mankind. Rather, the relationship is foundational to the purpose; both are essential keys to prayer.

THE MEANING OF DOMINION

The Earthly Realm

What does it mean for humanity to have dominion over the world? First, God has entrusted the care of the earth to man. This means that man is to be the proprietor of the physical earth, including all the other living things in the world—fish, birds, livestock, all the animals. In Genesis 2, we read that Adam was placed in the Garden of Eden to tend and cultivate it. This is what mankind is to do with the entire earth: both tend it and cultivate it. God told humanity, in effect, "Rule over My world. Take care of it. Subdue it and fashion it with your own creativity." Man has been given the freedom by God to exhibit creativity while governing the physical earth and all the other living things that dwell in it. The earth is to be ruled over, taken care of, fashioned, and molded by beings made in the image of their Creator.

---

[*] For more on the distinct designs of the male and female and their dominion roles, please refer to the author's books *Understanding the Purpose and Power of Woman* and *Understanding the Purpose and Power of Men,* both published by Whitaker House.

Man is meant to reflect the loving and creative Spirit of God.

This brings us to an interesting fact that many believers overlook today. God didn't originally create man for heaven; He created man for the earth. God is the Ruler of heaven, and He made man to express His authority in this world. He said, in effect, "I want what's happening in heaven to happen in the created world; I want My rule to extend to another realm, but I don't want to do it directly. I want man to share My rule."

God's plan for creation was this: as God ruled the unseen realm in heaven, man would rule the visible realm on earth, with God and man enjoying continual communion through their spiritual natures. In fact, God said something astounding about mankind, which is recorded in the Psalms: *"You are 'gods'; you are all sons of the Most High"* (Ps. 82:6). God has made us in His likeness and given each of us free will as a reflection of His own nature. He has created us to be His offspring. Therefore, He calls us "little gods."

God didn't create man for heaven. He created man for the earth.

Now, this does not mean that we are equal to God or that we are deity. Adam and Eve could fulfill their purpose only if they were relying on, and in constant communion with, the God of the Garden. Similarly, we can function in the purposes for which we were created only as we are connected to our Source. However, we need to recognize the high esteem and purposes God has for us. God said to man, in essence, "Let Me rule through you so you can appreciate, enjoy, and share in My governance."

The Spiritual Realm

Yet having dominion means even more than taking care of the physical world. Since man is both physical and spiritual in nature, humanity is meant to carry out God's purposes for the earth not only in the physical realm, but also in the spiritual realm. In this way, he is to spread the nature and character of God throughout the earth.

When God created Adam and Eve and placed them in the Garden of Eden, it was never His intention that they leave the Garden. Instead, He wanted the *Garden to be spread over the earth.* What does this mean? God wanted them to take the character of the Garden—God's presence, light, and truth—and spread it throughout the world. This was the overarching meaning of having dominion over the earth. This is still God's purpose. Isaiah 11:9 says, *"The earth will be full of the knowledge of the LORD as the waters cover the sea."*

Working with God rather than for God

When God created man to share His authority, it was in the context of humanity's relationship to Him as His offspring. God didn't create men and women to be servants, but to be sons and daughters who are wholeheartedly involved in running the family business. This was His plan for mankind from the beginning. He has always wanted His children to help Him fulfill His purposes.

This means that God doesn't want man to work *for* Him, but rather *with* Him. The Bible says that we are *"God's fellow workers"* (2 Cor. 6:1) or *"workers together with Him"* (NKJV). In the original Greek, *"fellow workers"* means those who "cooperate," who "help with," who "work together." We should always think of humanity's dominion in the context of a joint purpose with God based on mutual love and of the relationship of sons and daughters to their heavenly Father.

Let's summarize what we've discussed up to this point:

- God is a God of purpose, and His purposes are eternal.
- God desired offspring who would be like Him and who would share His rulership and dominion.
- God created humanity with and for a desired purpose.
- God created mankind in His image and likeness, as a reflection of His own nature.
- God made mankind with a sovereign will and with a capacity for creative expression.
- Carrying out God's purpose and will on earth is man's vocation.

- Man is to carry out his dominion in both the physical and spiritual realms.
- To fulfill God's purpose, men and women must desire to do His will—not by working *for* Him as His servants but *with* Him as His offspring.
- Man can function in his purposes only as he is connected to his Source—to God as Creator and Father.

THE NATURE OF PRAYER

We know that tragedy came to mankind when Adam and Eve turned their backs on God and desired their own wills apart from His will. Some think prayer originated because we were separated from God by our sin, and we needed a means by which to reconnect with Him. That is one use for prayer; however, it is not the heart of prayer. To understand its essence, we must realize that prayer began with the *creation* of mankind. It was not instituted after the Fall but before it. Prayer existed from the beginning of God's relationship with man.

Prayer Is the Expression of Man's Relationship with God and Participation in His Purposes

The true nature of prayer can be understood only in the context of God's purposes for humanity, which we have just discussed. The essence of prayer is twofold.

Prayer is—
an expression of mankind's unity and relationship
of love with God.
an expression of mankind's affirmation of and participation
in God's purposes for the earth.

To pray means to commune with God, to become one with God. It means union with Him—unity and singleness of purpose, thought, desire, will, reason, motive, objective, and feelings. H. D. Bollinger said, "Prayer is a being expressing relationship with another being."

Therefore, prayer is man's vehicle of the soul and spirit by which he communes with the invisible God. It is also the medium through which the human spirit affects and is affected by the will and purpose of the divine Creator. Therefore, we can also say,

> **Prayer is the involvement of oneself (one's whole self) with God.**

Who prayed the first prayer? I would say that it was Adam, since he was created first and was the one to whom God first spoke concerning how to tend the Garden and the parameters of mankind's authority on earth (Gen. 2:15–17). The Bible implies that God made a practice of walking and talking with Adam in the cool of the day (Gen. 3:8–9). The fellowship between God and Adam, and Adam's agreement with God's purposes, formed the essence of the first prayer. You may say, "Yes, but Adam was already in the presence of God. Why did he need to pray?"

Because of the fall of mankind (see Genesis 3), and because of the stubbornness of our sinful nature, we often need to prepare our hearts in prayer so we can truly enter God's presence. Yet that is only for the purpose of taking us where we were originally created to be, the place where Adam and Eve were before the Fall—a place of purity before God in which we reflect His nature and a oneness with His purposes, in which our wills are in total agreement with His will. Jesus said, *"Where two or three come together in my name, there am I with them"* (Matt. 18:20). The heart of prayer is communion with God in a unity of love and purpose. It is agreeing with God—heart, soul, mind, and strength—to bring about God's will.

The heart of prayer is communion with God in a unity of love and purpose.

Prayer Is Not Optional

This brings us back to the question we asked at the beginning of this chapter: Why do we have to ask God to do what He has already determined to do? The answer relates to God's faithfulness to His own Word and His integrity never to break that Word—because His Word is His name; it is who He is. He had said, *"Let us make man in our image, in our likeness, and let them rule ["have dominion" KJV]... over all the earth"* (Gen. 1:26). When God gave man dominion, He gave him the freedom to legally function as the authority on this planet. In this way, He placed His will for the earth on the cooperation of the will of man. God did not change this purpose when mankind fell, because His purposes are eternal. *"The plans of the LORD stand firm forever, the purposes of his heart through all generations"* (Ps. 33:11).

In the next chapter, we will see how Christ became the Second Adam and redeemed mankind so that humanity might be fully restored to a relationship of love with God and participation in His purposes for the earth. Yet even before God's plan of redemption was fully accomplished in Christ, God used humans to fulfill His will. We see this truth worked out in the lives of Abraham, Moses, Gideon, David, Daniel, and many others. God continued to work with mankind to fulfill His purposes on earth even though man's part was now limited by his sin and lack of understanding of God's ways.

Therefore, our need for prayer is a result of the way God arranged dominion and authority for the earth. God made the world. Then He made men and women and gave them dominion over all the works of His hands. Man was created to be the "god" of this world. He was given full authority in the earth realm, and God will not supercede that authority. This means that when God said, *"Let them rule...over all the earth,"* He was ordering the dominion of the world in such a way as to make the rule of humans essential for the accomplishment of His purposes. He causes things to happen on earth when men and women are in agreement with His will. Prayer, therefore, is essential for God's will to be done in the earth. Since God never breaks His Word concerning how things are to work, prayer is mandatory (not optional) for spiritual progress and victory in our individual lives and in the world at large.

God's plan is for man to desire what He desires, to will what He wills, and to ask Him to accomplish His purposes in the world so that goodness and truth may reign on the earth rather than evil and darkness. In this sense, prayer is man giving God the freedom to intervene in earth's affairs. In other words,

Prayer is earthly license for heavenly interference.

PURPOSE IS THE RAW MATERIAL OF PRAYER

As a member of the human race created in the image of God, this dominion authority is your heritage. God's desire is for you to will His will. His will is meant to be the backbone and center of your prayers, the heart of your intercession, the source of your confidence in supplication, the strength of your fervent and effectual prayers.

Praying does not mean convincing God to do your will, but doing His will through your will. Therefore, the key to effective prayer is understanding God's purpose for your life, His reason for your existence—as a human being in general and as an individual specifically. This is an especially important truth to remember: *Once you understand your purpose, it becomes the "raw material," the foundational matter, for your prayer life.* God's will is the authority of your prayers. Prayer is calling forth what God has already purposed and predestined—continuing His work of creation and the establishment of His plans for the earth.

In this way, your purpose in God is the foundational material for your prayers regarding—

provision
healing
deliverance
power
protection
endurance
patience

authority

faith

praise

thanksgiving

confidence

assurance

boldness

peace

—for the supply of all your needs. We will take an in-depth look at this essential truth in a later chapter.

Everything you need is available to fulfill your purpose. All that God is, and all that He has, may be received through prayer. The measure of our appropriation of God's grace is determined by the measure of our prayers.

GOD'S WILL IS THE CONFIDENCE OF OUR PRAYERS

Some people say, "I'm not entirely sure what I'm supposed to pray for." The answer is found in our purpose. We are not to ask God to do anything outside of what we have been given to do based on our purpose. We will be discussing the practical application of this truth throughout the rest of this book. We keep praying amiss because we continue to ask for the wrong things. *"When you ask, you do not receive, because you ask with wrong motives, that you may spend what you get on your pleasures"* (James 4:3). If we ask for things that are contrary to our purpose, we will be frustrated. Jesus always prayed for God's will to be done, and then worked to accomplish it.

All that God is, and all that God has, may be received through prayer.

For example, one of the longest recorded prayers is in John 17. Jesus' prayer, in effect, was this: "Father, before I came to earth, You gave Me people to redeem. I have protected them, I have kept them safe for that purpose, and now I am going to effect that redemption through My death and resurrection. I have fulfilled and am about to fulfill Your purpose for Me." (See John 17:6, 9–12.) Jesus knew the heavenly Father's purpose for His life, and He both desired to do the will of God and acted on it. *"'My food,' said Jesus, 'is to do the will of him who sent me and to finish his work'"* (John 4:34).

In John 11:41–42, Jesus expressed His confidence that God heard His prayers.

> *Then Jesus looked up and said, "Father, I thank you that you have heard me. I knew that you always hear me, but I said this for the benefit of the people standing here, that they may believe that you sent me."*

Jesus' assurance in prayer was based on His knowing and doing God's will. As it says in 1 John:

> *This is the confidence we have in approaching God: that if we ask anything according to his will, he hears us. And if we know that he hears us—whatever we ask—we know that we have what we asked of him.*
> (1 John 5:14–15)

PRAYER IS EXERCISING THE AUTHORITY OF DOMINION

When we know God's will, when we are obedient to it, and when we ask God to fulfill it, God will grant what we ask of Him. Whether we are praying for individual, family, community, national, or world needs, we must seek to be in agreement with God's will so that His purposes can reign in the earth. This is the essence of exercising dominion.

When we pray, we carry out our responsibility to demonstrate what our relationship with the Lord means in terms of living and ruling in the world. Since He has given humanity authority over the earth, He requires the permission or authorization of mankind in order to act on the earth. This is why, when we stop praying, we allow God's purposes for the world to be hindered. Recall that Jesus taught His disciples *"that they should always pray and not give up"* (Luke 18:1). He also said, *"I will give you the keys of the kingdom of heaven; whatever you bind on earth will be bound in heaven, and whatever you loose on earth will be loosed in heaven"* (Matt. 16:19).

These truths are crucial for effective prayer. We need to ask God to intervene in human affairs. If we don't, our world will be susceptible to the influences of Satan and sin. God will ultimately bring His purposes to pass in the world—with or without our cooperation. If you do not pray, He will eventually find someone who will agree with His plans. However, when you neglect to pray, you are failing to fulfill *your* role in His purposes. He does not want you to miss out on this privilege—for your sake, as well as His. James 4:2 says, *"You do not have, because you do not ask God."*

Prayer is not an option for the believer. It is a necessity to fulfill God's purposes in the world and in our individual lives. Time spent in prayer is not time wasted but time invested. As we embrace the will of God, as we live before Him in the righteousness of Christ, as we seek to fulfill His purposes, nothing will be able to hinder our prayers, and we will begin to understand Jesus' saying, *"With God all things are possible"* (Matt. 19:26).

BROKEN RELATIONSHIP WITH GOD MEANS BROKEN EFFECTIVENESS IN PRAYER

God gave humanity a vast amount of freedom and authority on earth. Yet these gifts were dependent on man's using his will to do the will of God. If he used his will for anything other than God's will, the image and likeness of God within him would be marred, and the purposes of God for the world would be obstructed—purposes of goodness, fruitfulness, creativity, truth, joy, and love. The rebellion of the first man and woman brought about this distortion of God's image in mankind and thus attacked God's plans for the earth. This happened because man used his will for self-serving purposes, whereas God's will is based on love.

How did this rebellion come about? Satan tempted Adam and Eve to disobey God, and they chose to agree with his purposes rather than with God's. In doing so, mankind sinned and cut off communion with God. Humanity no longer agreed with God to fulfill His purposes for earth—leaving the world at the mercy of a renegade authority that no longer had God's best interests in mind. In fact, man forfeited his authority to Satan, whom he had chosen to serve in place of God. That meant that the Fall introduced a new ruler on earth—one bent on its destruction rather than its growth in godliness and fruitfulness. Because Satan usurped mankind's authority on earth, the apostle Paul referred to him as *"the god of this world"* (2 Cor. 4:4 KJV).

When Adam and Eve broke their relationship with God, their effectiveness in prayer was also broken. True prayer is maintained through oneness of heart and purpose with God. Only then can we fulfill God's ways and plans. When we pray, we represent God's interests on earth, and representation requires relationship. Therefore, our difficulties with prayer may be traced to the Fall and the resulting fallen nature of man, through which we were estranged from God. Even as redeemed believers, we must realize and act upon who we are in Christ and the principles of prayer that God has established, if we are to be restored to His purposes in the crucial area of prayer.

We may not think of prayer as being an area in which we need to be *"transformed by the renewing of* [our] *mind"* (Rom. 12:2 KJV). However, since effective prayer has everything to do with being united with God in a relationship of love, having a heart and mind in union with God's will, gaining a discerning mind in regard to His purposes, and exercising faith in His Word, it is a vital area in which we need to be transformed. Prayer should not be open-ended. It should be purpose-driven, motivated by a knowledge of God's ways and intentions.

> **Prayer should be purpose-driven, motivated by a knowledge of God's will.**

GOD'S PURPOSE FOR MANKIND IS ETERNAL

The full text of 2 Corinthians 4:4 says, *"The god of this world hath blinded the minds of them which believe not, lest the light of the glorious gospel of Christ, who is the image of*

God, should shine unto them" (KJV). It is interesting to note that, in the original Greek, one meaning of the word *"world"* in this verse is "a space of time" and "an age." In fact, some Bible versions translate the first part of the verse as *"the god of this age"* (NIV, NKJV). Perhaps the use of this term was meant to emphasize the fact that Satan may be the god of this world now—but he won't be forever. His reign will last only for a time, only for a specific age. God's purposes are eternal, and He had a plan in mind from the foundation of the world to restore mankind to Himself so that our spirits and our minds could be fully renewed in God. *"God...has saved us and called us to a holy life—not because of anything we have done but because of his own purpose and grace. This grace was given us in Christ Jesus before the beginning of time"* (2 Tim. 1:8–9). *"He chose us in him before the creation of the world to be holy and blameless in his sight. In love he predestined us to be adopted as his sons through Jesus Christ, in accordance with his pleasure and will"* (Eph. 1:4–5).

God's plan was for mankind to be restored and the earth to be renewed through a new Ruler—the Second Adam, fully human yet fully divine—who would be perfectly one with God and His purposes: *"the man Christ Jesus"* (1 Tim. 2:5).

> *For to us a child is born, to us a son is given, and the government will be on his shoulders. And he will be called Wonderful Counselor, Mighty God, Everlasting Father, Prince of Peace. Of the increase of his government and peace there will be no end. He will reign on David's throne and over his kingdom, establishing and upholding it with justice and righteousness from that time on and forever. The zeal of the Lord Almighty will accomplish this.* (Isa. 9:6–7)

In the next chapter, we will see how Christ reestablished mankind's authority in the world and restored to us the purpose and power of prayer.

LET'S PRAY TOGETHER

Heavenly Father,

You have said, *"Many are the plans in a man's heart, but it is the Lord's purpose that prevails"* (Prov. 19:21). We ask you to fulfill Your word and make Your purpose reign in our lives. We all have plans and goals that we are pursuing. We ask you to establish whatever is from You—whatever is in line with Your purpose—and cause to fade away whatever is not from You. We honor you as our Creator and as our loving heavenly Father. We affirm that it is You who work in us to will and to act according to Your good purpose (Phil. 2:13). Renew our minds so we may understand Your ways and Your plans more fully. We pray this in the name of Jesus, who is our Way, Truth, and Life. Amen.

PUTTING PRAYER INTO PRACTICE

Ask yourself:

- Have I ever neglected to pray because I felt God would do whatever He wanted to do anyway?
- If the real purpose of prayer is to fulfill God's purposes on earth, how much do I know about those purposes? How can I learn more about what God's purposes are?
- Have I been resisting God's will in any area of my life?
- What can I do today to build a deeper relationship of love with God?
- What is one of God's purposes that I can begin to agree with Him about in prayer today?

Principles

1. God is a God of purpose, and His purposes are eternal.
2. God created mankind for and with a desired purpose.
3. God desired offspring with whom He could share a relationship of love, as well as rulership and dominion.
4. God created mankind in His image, with His nature and moral character, and with a sovereign will.
5. God gave mankind the freedom to function as the legal authority on earth. He placed His will for the earth on the cooperation of man's will. This purpose never changed, even after the fall of mankind.
6. God's will is His purpose for mankind. To fulfill what they were created to be and do, men and women must desire to do God's will.
7. Prayer is an expression of mankind's unity and relationship of love with God. It is also an expression of mankind's affirmation of and participation in God's purposes.
8. Prayer is the involvement of one's whole self with God.
9. Prayer is the medium through which the human spirit affects and is affected by the will and purpose of the divine Creator.
10. Prayer is not optional. It is essential for the fulfillment of God's purposes on earth.
11. Prayer is man giving God the freedom to intervene in earth's affairs.
12. When we know God's purpose and will, when we are obedient to it, and when we ask God to fulfill it, God will grant what we ask of Him.
13. When Adam and Eve broke their relationship with God, their effectiveness in prayer was also broken. True prayer is maintained through oneness of heart and purpose with God.

Chapter Three

The Authority of Prayer

The position and authority that Jesus won have been transferred back to mankind through spiritual rebirth in Christ.

What gives you the right to pray? Becoming sure of the answer to that question in your own heart and mind is essential if you are to have an effective prayer life. In the last chapter, we saw that God instituted prayer when He created mankind. We learned that—

Prayer is the vehicle by which you are meant to commune with the invisible God. It is the medium through which your spirit is intended to affect and be affected by the will and purpose of the divine Creator.

That's the *purpose* of prayer. However, on what basis do you have a *right* to pray?

God originally gave us this right by virtue of our relationship with Him and our purpose of exercising dominion over the earth. Yet our relationship with our Creator was broken, and our dominion authority was forfeited by our first ancestors. Satan, rather than man, became *"the god of this world"* (2 Cor. 4:4 KJV).

Where did this leave people in relation to communion with God and His purposes for prayer? They became estranged from Him and His plans for them, so that they—

- felt isolated from God.
- were unsure of where they stood with God.
- didn't know what God wanted to do for and through them.
- lost their sense of purpose.

Do these results sound at all like your own prayer life? If so, you must realize that your concept of prayer has been influenced by the effects of the Fall. However, God wants to give you a new outlook on prayer, one that reflects His purposes for redemption as well as creation.

GOD'S PLAN OF REDEMPTION IS CONSISTENT WITH HIS CHARACTER AND PURPOSES

We have seen that God's purposes are eternal and that He had a plan in place since the foundation of the world for the restoration of mankind. Note that this restoration, which involved defeating Satan and sin, was accomplished in line with God's principles. His purposes never changed. God's plan was not simply to come down and wrench control of the earth back from Satan. He *could* have done that, but He never *would* have done it. Why? It would have been inconsistent with the integrity of His character and His purposes. If He had done that, Satan could have accused Him of doing what he had done—usurping the authority that had been given to man in creation.

God respected man's authority even when it lay dormant within his fallen nature.

God has *all* power and authority. Yet He has given mankind authority over the earth, as well as a free will, and He will not rescind those gifts—even though man sinned, rejected Him, and deserved to be separated from Him forever. Scripture says, *"For the wages of sin is death"* (Rom. 6:23). What extraordinary respect God has for humanity! He respected the authority of man even when it lay dormant within his fallen nature, for *"God's gifts and his call are irrevocable"* (Rom. 11:29).

Yet how could God enable humanity to regain a relationship with Him and authority on the earth when man had thrown away these gifts by his own choice? We need to appreciate the magnitude of man's dilemma. Man's sin would have to be dealt with. Man would also have to want to return to God and work together with Him of his own free will. These were no simple matters. Restoring mankind

48

would have been impossible if it were not for Christ. As Jesus Himself said, *"With man this is impossible, but with God all things are possible"* (Matt. 19:26). God's eternal plan for humanity was made possible through the coming of Jesus Christ. Only through Christ are we restored to our purposes in God, and *only through Christ do we have a right to pray with authority.*

CHRIST RESTORED OUR RIGHTS TO DOMINION AND PRAYER

Again, from the beginning God planned for man's redemption and restoration of purpose to come through Jesus.

> [God] *made known to us the mystery of his will according to his good pleasure, which he purposed in Christ....His intent was that now, through the church, the manifold wisdom of God should be made known to the rulers and authorities in the heavenly realms, according to his eternal purpose which he accomplished in Christ Jesus our Lord. In him and through faith in him we may approach God with freedom and confidence.* (Eph. 1:9; 3:10–12)

Jesus Is the Second Adam

How could Christ accomplish God's *"eternal purpose"* (Eph. 3:11)? To restore God's purpose, Jesus had to come as a Representative of the legal authority of the earth—man. He had to come as a *human being,* as the Second Adam, as the beginning of a new family of mankind who would be devoted to God—*"the firstborn among many brothers"* (Rom. 8:29). Scripture says, *"The Word became flesh and made his dwelling among us"* (John 1:14). If He had not come as a man, He would not have had the right to reclaim humanity and the earth for God, according to the way God has ordered His purposes for the world.

Also, to restore man's broken relationship with God, Jesus had to be without sin, and He had to *choose* to do the will of God. Only a perfectly righteous man who desired to do God's will could redeem humanity. The Bible says, *"God made him who had no sin to be sin for us, so that in him we*

49

might become the righteousness of God" (2 Cor. 5:21). Therefore, the second person of the Trinity voluntarily put aside His heavenly glory and came to earth as a man:

> [Christ], *being in very nature God, did not consider equality with God something to be grasped, but made himself nothing, taking the very nature of a servant, being made in human likeness. And being found in appearance as a man, he humbled himself and became obedient to death—even death on a cross!*
> (Phil. 2:6–8)

> *For what the law was powerless to do in that it was weakened by the sinful nature, God did by sending his own Son in the likeness of sinful man to be a sin offering. And so he condemned sin in sinful man, in order that the righteous requirements of the law might be fully met in us, who do not live according to the sinful nature but according to the Spirit.*
> (Rom. 8:3–4)

What qualities did Christ manifest as the Second Adam?

He Is the Image of God

First, Jesus reflected God's image, as Adam had originally done. Jesus is called *"Christ, who is the image of God"* (2 Cor. 4:4).

Moreover, the second person of the Trinity retained His divinity, so that Christ is both fully human and fully God. This means that the fullness of the *"image of God"* was revealed in both His humanity and His divinity: *"God was pleased to have all his fullness dwell in him"* (Col. 1:19). *"For in Christ all the fullness of the Deity lives in bodily form, and you have been given fullness in Christ, who is the head over every power and authority"* (Col. 2:9–10). *"He is the image of the invisible God, the firstborn over all creation"* (Col. 1:15).

He Has a Deep Relationship of Love with God

Jesus also has a unique relationship of love with God the Father, perfectly reflecting the relationship God desired to have with Adam and Eve. *"The Father loves the Son and has placed everything in his hands"* (John 3:35). *"For the Father loves the Son and shows him all he does"* (John 5:20). *"The reason my Father loves me is that I lay down my life—only to take it up again"* (John 10:17). The love of the Father and the Son is so deep and reciprocal that Jesus could say, *"I and the Father are one"* (v. 30).

He Lives to Do God's Will

The above verses remind us of the connection between love for God and oneness with His purposes, which was characteristic of humanity's original relationship with God. Throughout the Gospels, Jesus revealed that His one purpose and objective in life was to do the will of God:

> *Going a little farther, he fell with his face to the ground and prayed, "My Father, if it is possible, may this cup be taken from me. Yet not as I will, but as you will.*"...*He went away a second time and prayed, "My Father, if it is not possible for this cup to be taken away unless I drink it, may your will be done."*
> (Matt. 26:39, 42)

> *Your kingdom come. Your will be done on earth as it is in heaven.* (Luke 11:2 NKJV)

> *"My food," said Jesus, "is to do the will of him who sent me and to finish his work."* (John 4:34)

> *I can of Myself do nothing. As I hear, I judge; and My judgment is righteous, because I do not seek My own will but the will of the Father who sent Me.* (John 5:30 NKJV)

> *For I have come down from heaven not to do my will but to do the will of him who sent me.* (John 6:38)

Jesus lives to do the will of God. He is one with God and His purposes, and He said that anyone who does God's will belongs to the family of God: *"Whoever does the will of my Father in heaven is my brother and sister and mother"* (Matt. 12:50).

He Reigns with Authority

Just as Adam and Eve were meant to administer God's rule on earth, Christ exhibited the authority of God while He lived on the earth: *"The blind receive sight, the lame walk, those who have leprosy are cured, the deaf hear, the dead are raised, and the good news is preached to the poor"* (Matt. 11:5). Moreover, His authority and reign were powerfully manifested when He rose from the dead and conquered sin, Satan, and death. When He returns to earth, His authority will be recognized by the whole world:

> *At the name of Jesus every knee should bow, in heaven and on earth and under the earth, and every tongue confess that Jesus Christ is Lord, to the glory of God the Father.* (Phil. 2:10–11)

> *On his robe and on his thigh he has this name written: KING OF KINGS AND LORD OF LORDS.* (Rev. 19:16)

> *The kingdom of the world has become the kingdom of our Lord and of his Christ, and he will reign for ever and ever.* (Rev. 11:15)

Jesus has the right and the power to reign on the earth and to ask God to intervene in the world since He was the perfect Man and the perfect Sacrifice. This means that even if no other men are in agreement with God, God's purposes for the earth can be brought about in Christ. His prayers for mankind are powerful and effective. *"Therefore he is able to save completely those who come to God through him, because he always lives to intercede for them"* (Heb. 7:25). In addition, He has given believers His Spirit so that we can agree with God's purposes even when we are uncertain about how to pray. *"In the same way, the Spirit helps us in our weakness. We do not know what we ought to pray for, but the Spirit himself intercedes for us with groans that words cannot express"* (Rom. 8:26).

As lawful King of the earth, Jesus ultimately has the right to silence anyone who opposes God. Mankind has been given free will by God. Yet as humanity's Redeemer and King,

Christ is qualified to be the Judge of all mankind. Through Christ, man is judged by one of his own. Jesus said, *"The Father judges no one, but has entrusted all judgment to the Son"* (John 5:22).

Jesus Reclaimed Mankind's Earthly Authority

Christ accomplished our redemption and reclaimed our earthly authority as a result of His being the Second Adam. It is crucial for us to remember that—

- Jesus came as a man. Thus, He was qualified as a Representative of earthly authority.
- Jesus was perfectly obedient and sinless. Thus, He was qualified to be the Son of God and to restore man's relationship with the Father by overcoming sin and death through His sacrifice on the cross.
- Jesus rose victoriously. Thus, He was qualified to defeat sin and Satan, regain authority over the earth, and be the earth's rightful King.

Jesus Transferred Authority to Those Who Believe

There is a vital relationship between redemption and true prayer. The position and authority that Jesus won have been transferred back to mankind through spiritual rebirth in Christ (John 3:5). Those who believe and receive Christ have their relationship with God and their authority on earth restored. Because of Christ, we can live again as true sons and daughters of God, with all the rights and privileges associated with being His offspring. Prayer is both a right and a privilege of redeemed man, who is now in a position to enter fully into a relationship of love with God and to agree that "His kingdom come, His will be done on earth as it is in heaven." (See Matthew 6:10.)

Prayer is both a right and a privilege of redeemed man.

It is God's will that every person be redeemed and rule the earth through the Spirit of Christ. It is through mankind that God desires to reveal His character, nature, principles, precepts, and righteousness to the visible world.

This is an *eternal* plan. It applies to our present lives on earth, and it will apply throughout eternity.

Remember that it was never God's intention that man would live and work in heaven; he was created for earth. Because of the Fall, our spirits will now separate from our bodies at death, and the redeemed will go to be with God in heaven. Yet God made us a promise. He said that when we come to the head office (heaven), we will stay there only for a while. There will come a Day when our bodies will be resurrected and rejoined with our spirits, so that we can continue to rule—in the new earth God will create. (See 1 Corinthians 15:42–44, 51–53; Isaiah 65:17.)

In the book of Revelation, God speaks of thrones, and of our reigning and ruling with Him on earth. (See Revelation 5:10; 20:4, 6; 22:5.) Again, God isn't going to raise you from the dead just to live with Him forever. He's going to raise you so that you can get on with your work—your calling and vocation. That is why Scripture says that we will reign with Jesus. *"They will reign for ever and ever"* (Rev. 22:5). *Reign* means what? To have dominion, to administrate.

Therefore, as we live and work in this fallen world today and, in the future, when we will live and reign with Jesus, the commission from God is the same: *"Let them rule...over all the earth"* (Gen. 1:26).

MAN'S REDEMPTION ALLOWS HIM TO HAVE DOMINION

Many believers could not be described as *"having dominion"* in the sense of making a meaningful contribution to furthering the kingdom of God on earth. What prevents us from doing this? Often it is because we do not recognize—or accept—our calling and authority, which we have received in Christ. We do not know our rights based on the *"new covenant"*:

> *Not that we are competent in ourselves to claim anything for ourselves, but our competence comes from God. He has made us competent as ministers of a new covenant—not of the letter but of the Spirit; for the letter kills, but the Spirit gives life.* (2 Cor. 3:5–6)

I believe that our fear of being proud or presumptuous, along with our lack of acceptance of our worth in Christ, have kept us in bondage and robbed us of the reality of His finished work on our behalf. How slow we have been to act on what we are in Christ! Yet He wants us to use what He has made available for us through redemption.

For example, because the church has not understood the true nature of humility, we have been taught for so long and so persistently about our weaknesses, our lack of ability, and our un-worthiness that we hardly dare to affirm what God says we are: *"a new creation"* (2 Cor. 5:17). We are afraid that if we do, people will misunderstand us and think we have become fanatical. Yet the Scripture says, *"If anyone is in Christ, he is a new creation; the old has gone, the new has come! All this is from God"* (vv. 17–18). This is not something we have made up. It is not presumption on our part. It is from God. Therefore, we don't have to be afraid to say it and to live in its wonderful reality.

> **We have been taught for so long about our weaknesses and unworthiness that we hardly dare to affirm that we are *"a new creation."***

The Spirit has declared what this new creation entails. It includes everything that we are in Christ. Ephesians 1:7 says, *"In him we have redemption through his blood, the for-giveness of sins, in accordance with the riches of God's grace."*

Who are we in Christ? We are the redeemed. Again, this is not just a philosophy or an opinion. This is the Father's description of who we are in His Son. The Second Adam re-deemed mankind. Therefore, not only are we a new crea-tion, but we also have a redemption that is literal and absolute.

What does this redemption mean to us?

Satan Has No Authority over Us

Satan is the prince of darkness, and he became the god of this world when he successfully tempted Adam and Eve to reject God's ways. Yet through Christ, we have been delivered from Satan's dominion, out of the realm of darkness. That is why, even though we continue to live in a fallen world, we do not belong to it. We belong to God's kingdom: *"He has rescued us from the dominion of darkness and brought us into the kingdom of the Son he loves"* (Col. 1:13). *"But you are a chosen people, a royal priesthood, a holy nation, a people belonging to God, that you may declare the praises of him who called you out of darkness into his wonderful light"* (1 Pet. 2:9). Because we have been delivered from Satan's dominion, he no longer has authority over us. Rather, we have authority over him in the name of Jesus.

Sin Has No Authority over Us

Christ has also delivered us from the dominion and power of sin. *"Sin shall not be your master, because you are not under law, but under grace"* (Rom. 6:14). The Bible says that when we have repented of our sins and believed in Jesus as our Substitute and Representative, we are *"in Christ"* (2 Cor. 5:17). We are *"the righteousness of God"* in Him (v. 21). Since He is sinless, we, also, are free from sin. We may not appreciate or appropriate this fact, but it is still true. *"Where sin increased, grace increased all the more, so that, just as sin reigned in death, so also grace might reign through righteousness to bring eternal life through Jesus Christ our Lord"* (Rom. 5:20–21). Therefore, because of redemption, sin no longer reigns in our lives— grace does.

We Have Authority through Jesus' Name

Our redemption has also given us authority in Jesus' name. Jesus clearly stated,

> I tell you the truth, anyone who has faith in me will do what I have been doing. He will do even greater things than these, because I am going to the Father. And I will do whatever you ask in my name, so that the Son may bring glory to the Father. You may ask me for anything in my name, and I will do it. (John 14:12–14)

I tell you the truth, my Father will give you whatever you ask in my name. Until now you have not asked for anything in my name. Ask and you will receive, and your joy will be complete. (John 16:23–24)

A major principle regarding our authority and power in prayer is our right to use the name of Jesus. We will look more closely at this principle in a later chapter.

We Have Access to the Father through Jesus' Name

The authority of Jesus' name gives us access to our heavenly Father. Our right to *"approach the throne of grace with confidence"* (Heb. 4:16) brings us the delight of a restored relationship with God. Yet this essential aspect of prayer also enables us to agree with the Father and His purposes, and to ask Him to fulfill His Word as He meets our needs and the needs of others.

In that day you will ask in my name. I am not saying that I will ask the Father on your behalf. No, the Father himself loves you because you have loved me and have believed that I came from God.
(John 16:26–27)

We Have Authority through the Word

God's presence, power, and unlimited resources are available to us in the name of Jesus. Yet Jesus' name isn't a magic word we use to get what we want. We must pray according to God's will, which we find in His Word. Jesus said in John 15:7, *"If you remain in me and my words remain in you, ask whatever you wish, and it will be given you."* The backbone of prayer is our agreement with God's Word, our oneness with Christ, who is the Living Word, and our unity with God's purposes and will.

Power in prayer is not based on feelings but on the Word of God.

Power in prayer is not based on emotions, feelings, or the theories of men, but upon the Word of God, *"which lives and abides forever"* (1 Pet. 1:23 NKJV). His Word is the guarantee of answered prayer. God is asking you to bring Him His Word, to plead your covenant rights. We are not to pray to God in ignorance but as partners in His purposes. Prayer is joining forces with God the Father by calling attention to His promises. *"No matter how many promises God has made, they are 'Yes' in Christ. And so through him the 'Amen' is spoken by us to the glory of God"* (2 Cor. 1:20). The *New King James Version* expresses it in this way: *"For all the promises of God in Him are Yes, and in Him Amen, to the glory of God through us."*

Since appropriating the promises of God is another major principle with regard to our authority and power in prayer, we will be taking a closer look at this principle in a subsequent chapter.

JESUS IS OUR MODEL OF DOMINION AUTHORITY

Jesus is not only the One who reclaimed our dominion authority, but He is also our model for how we are to live in this authority. He was what we are to be. His prayer life is an example of the prayer life we are to have.

You may say, "Yes, but Jesus was different from us. He was divine, and so He had an advantage over us."

When Jesus was on earth, was He in a better position than we are? No. What He accomplished on earth, He accomplished in His humanity, not His divinity. Otherwise, He could not have been man's Representative and Substitute. As the Son of Man, Jesus kept a close relationship with the Father through prayer. He did what God directed Him to do and what He saw God actively working to accomplish in the world. He relied on the grace and Spirit of God. We can do the same.

Jesus said,

> *My Father is always at his work to this very day, and I, too, am working....I tell you the truth, the Son can do nothing by himself; he can do only what he sees his Father doing, because whatever the Father does the Son also does. For the Father loves the Son and shows him all he does.* (John 5:17, 19–20)

God loved Jesus because He was perfectly obedient and lived to fulfill God's purposes. *"The reason my Father loves me is that I lay down my life—only to take it up again"* (John 10:17). God revealed to Jesus what He was doing in the world and how Jesus' ministry related to His overall purpose. I believe that God will do the same for us as we live and work in the Spirit of Christ.

> *The words I say to you are not just my own. Rather, it is the Father, living in me, who is doing his work. Believe me when I say that I am in the Father and the Father is in me; or at least believe on the evidence of the miracles themselves. I tell you the truth, anyone who has faith in me will do what I have been doing. He will do even greater things than these, because I am going to the Father. And I will do whatever you ask in my name, so that the Son may bring glory to the Father. You may ask me for anything in my name, and I will do it.*   (John 14:10–14)

Jesus' prayers were effective because He had a relationship with God, knew His purposes, and prayed according to God's will—according to what God had already spoken and promised to do. We are to imitate Him. More than that, we are to let His Spirit and attitude rule in our lives. *"Let this mind be in you which was also in Christ Jesus"* (Phil. 2:5 NKJV). We are to live in the new covenant that God has granted us in Christ, which restores us to oneness with God's heart and will: *"'This is the covenant I will make with the house of Israel after that time,' declares the LORD. 'I will put my law in their minds and write it on their hearts. I will be their God, and they will be my people'"* (Jer. 31:33).

RULING THROUGH THE SPIRIT OF CHRIST

My question at the beginning of this chapter was, What gives you the right to pray? It is not only your calling in creation, but also your redemption in Christ that gives you this right. This is a solid and life-changing truth. It takes away doubt, fear, uncertainty, and timidity in regard to prayer. Because of Christ, you no longer have to feel—

- isolated from God.
- unsure of where you stand with God.
- unclear about what God wants to do for and through you.
- purposeless.

Instead, you can have—

- a relationship of love with God the Father.
- the certainty of your redemption in Christ.
- an understanding of your calling and authority in Christ.
- a clear idea of God's purpose for your life.

God wants you to live confidently in the authority He has given you. Christ says,

> *I tell you the truth, whatever you bind on earth will be bound in heaven, and whatever you loose on earth will be loosed in heaven. Again, I tell you that if two of you on earth agree about anything you ask for, it will be done for you by my Father in heaven.*
> (Matt. 18:18–19)

ARE YOU WILLING?

Do you want God to bring about His purposes for your life and for our fallen world? You can invite Him to do so through prayer.

From Genesis to Revelation, God always found a human being to help Him accomplish His purposes. He comes to you now and asks, in effect, "Are you willing? Will you help Me fulfill My purposes for your life and for the earth? Or are you contented to live an unfulfilled existence and to let the influences of sin and Satan encroach upon our world? *'Who is he who will devote himself to be close to me?'* (Jer. 30:21)."

I pray that we will desire to be close to God, living in oneness with Him and His purposes and exercising the authority He has given us through the Spirit of Christ.

LET'S PRAY TOGETHER

Heavenly Father,

Thank You for never giving up on us but for redeeming us for Yourself and Your purposes through Jesus Christ, the Second Adam. Paul prayed in 2 Thessalonians 1:11, *"That our God may count you worthy of his calling, and that by his power he may fulfill every good purpose of yours and every act prompted by your faith."* We ask You to count us worthy of our calling and to enable us to fulfill Your purposes, through the grace, faith, and authority we have in Christ. We pray these things in the name of Jesus, our Redeemer and King. Amen.

PUTTING PRAYER INTO PRACTICE

Ask yourself:

- Do I ever feel isolated from God, unsure of where I stand with Him, and unclear about how I should pray?
- Am I praying based on the effects of the Fall or the effects of Christ's work of redemption on my behalf?

Action Steps:

- Begin today to apply the redemption of Christ to your prayer life by acknowledging Jesus' restoration of your relationship with the Father and your purpose of dominion.
- Remind yourself daily that your redemption means that Satan and sin no longer have authority over you, that you have authority and access to the Father through Jesus' name, and that you have authority through the Word of God.
- Start approaching God based on this promise: *"Let us then approach the throne of grace with confidence, so that we may receive mercy and find grace to help us in our time of need"* (Heb. 4:16).

Principles

1. God's plan of redemption is consistent with His character and purposes. He redeemed man while keeping man's free will and earthly authority intact.

2. Through Christ we are restored to our purpose, and through Him we have a right to pray with authority.

3. As the Second Adam, Christ is the image of God, exhibits a relationship of love with God, lives to do God's will, and reigns as King of the earth and Judge of mankind.

4. Christ reclaimed our earthly authority in these ways:

   • Jesus came as a man. Thus He was qualified as a Representative of earthly authority.

   • Jesus was perfectly obedient and sinless. Thus He was qualified to be the Son of God and to restore man's relationship with the Father by overcoming sin and death through His sacrifice on the cross.

   • Jesus rose victoriously. Thus He was qualified to defeat sin and Satan, regain authority over the earth, and be its rightful King.

5. The position and authority that Jesus won have been transferred back to mankind through spiritual rebirth in Christ (John 3:5).

6. When we do not live in our position of authority, it is because we do not recognize or accept our calling in Christ, because we do not know our covenant rights.

7. Man's redemption allows him to have dominion. This means that Satan and sin have no authority over us, we have authority and access to the Father through Jesus' name, and we have authority through the Word of God.

8. Jesus is our model of dominion authority. What He accomplished on earth, He accomplished in His humanity, even though He was also divine. He relied on the grace and Spirit of God, as we can.

9. Our right to pray comes from both our calling in creation and our redemption in Christ.

Part II

Preparing for Prayer

Chapter Four

How to Enter God's Presence

We must learn to enter God's presence with the right spirit, approach, and preparation so we can commune with Him and offer effective prayers as God's priests.

O nce we understand that the heart of prayer is communion with God in a unity of love and purpose, how do we begin to pray? Where do we start? We first need to learn how to enter God's presence with the right spirit, approach, and preparation so that we can have this communion with Him.

We're going to be looking at a passage in the Old Testament book of Leviticus to illustrate a New Testament principle: the priesthood of believers. Jesus said, *"Do not think that I have come to abolish the Law or the Prophets; I have not come to abolish them but to fulfill them"* (Matt. 5:17). The New Testament reveals the deeper spiritual meanings of Old Testament practices and rituals, which were fulfilled in Jesus Christ. (See Hebrews 8:5–6; 9:23.) It is important to understand these Old Testament practices so we can appreciate what their fulfillment in the New Testament means for our relationship with God now that we are redeemed in Christ.

REVERENCE FOR GOD

The term "entering into God's presence" is frequently used in the church today in reference to worship and prayer. However, in our casual, twenty-first-century Christianity, most of us don't understand what this concept really means. Even when we attempt to do so wholeheartedly, we still don't fully attain it. Why? Frankly, it is because we often do not have a genuine reverence for God. Here's just a small example. When I was growing up, if a person was wearing a hat when he walked past a church, he would take off his hat in respect for the place where God was worshipped. Of course, today, we say, "Well, that's unnecessary. It's the attitude that counts." Yet I think we have lost the attitude as well as the custom. We need to be spiritually sensitive to the fact that God is holy, mighty, and worthy to be reverenced.

One of the favorite theological ideas in many churches today is that grace cancels law. Yet because we misunderstand the nature of grace, we are casual about our obedience to God. We commit sin, and then we hurriedly ask for forgiveness on our way to church or prayer meeting. By the time we get to the door, we think we're ready to join with other believers in prayer. We treat the precious blood of Jesus, which He gave His life to deliver to us, as if it's some temporary covering for our messes so we can sin all over again. Sadly, we don't really love Jesus. We use Him. Then we wonder why God doesn't answer our prayers. The truth is that grace supersedes law in the sense that only the grace we receive in Christ enables us to *fulfill* God's law.

The grace we receive in Christ enables us to fulfill God's law.

Jesus told us that the greatest commandment of all is, *"Love the Lord your God with all your heart and with all your soul and with all your mind"* (Matt. 22:37). God is saying to the church, in essence, "Don't obey Me because of the things you want from Me. Obey Me because you love Me. *'If you love me, you will obey what I command'* (John 14:15). If you love Me, you won't need chastisement and discipline to do what I ask of you."

God doesn't want us to use Him merely as safety insurance from hell. He wants a relationship, not a religion. He wants to be a Father to us. He wants communion with us. Communion means intimacy with our heavenly Father through which we express our love for Him, find out His will, and then do it. It is entering into the very mind and heart of God, in order to become one with Him and His purposes. In this sense, drawing close to God is not as simple a matter as we generally think.

HOLINESS AND INTEGRITY

When we don't have a healthy fear of God or respect for His commandments, we are unable to truly enter His presence. That is why, when we talk about seeking God, we must talk about the word *holiness*. Holiness is critical to prayer because *"without holiness no one will see the Lord"* (Heb. 12:14). Jesus emphasized this truth when He said, *"Blessed are the pure in heart, for they will see God"* (Matt. 5:8). I don't believe these verses refer to seeing God in heaven after we die but to everyday life on earth. They refer to seeing God now, in the sense of having an intimate relationship of love with Him and entering into His presence so we can know His heart and mind.

Holiness is critical to prayer because *"without holiness no one will see the Lord."*

When Jesus said that the pure in heart will see God, it was during His first public teaching, found in Matthew 5. He taught the people what we now refer to as The Beatitudes, and what I like to call "the Attitudes to Be"—the attitudes that define who we are supposed to be in Christ. Jesus began by saying, "Blessed are the poor in spirit, for they shall inherit the kingdom of heaven. Blessed are those who mourn, who really seek after God." (See vv. 3–4.) To mourn means to humble yourself in fasting. Thus, Jesus said, *"Blessed are those who mourn, for they will be comforted"* (v. 4). God will satisfy you if you seek Him with all your heart. It was in this context that Jesus said, *"Blessed are the pure in heart, for they will see God"* (v. 8).

When Jesus made this statement, He wasn't referring to our dying and seeing God in heaven. He was teaching us the attitudes we are to live by every day—on this earth. He was telling us how to remain in unity with God.

What does it mean to be pure in heart? *Pure* means holy. Therefore, Jesus was saying, in effect, "Blessed are the holy in heart, for they will see God." The word *holy* means to "sanctify, or set apart," or "to be set." "Blessed are the set in heart, for they will see God." When you are pure in heart, your mind is set on God and His ways.

"I am the LORD your God; consecrate yourselves [set yourselves apart] *and be holy, because I am holy"* (Lev. 11:44). *"I am the LORD, who makes you holy"* (Lev. 20:8). There is perhaps no word that describes God better than *holiness*. In these verses, God is saying, "Set yourself in the same way that I set myself; be holy, just as I am holy." To consecrate yourself means to position or set yourself in such a way that you say, "I'm not going to stop until I get what I'm going after." Leviticus 20:26 says, *"You are to be holy to me because I, the LORD, am holy, and I have set you apart from the nations to be my own."* Holiness always has to do with separation. It has to do with fixing yourself on God and not being influenced by people who are not set on Him and who do not believe His Word.

What does it mean to "see" God in relation to prayer? The Scriptures say, *"Stand still, and see the salvation of the LORD"* (Exod. 14:13; 2 Chron. 20:17 NKJV). God says, in essence, "If you are holy, then I will manifest Myself to you. You will see Me; you will see My salvation in your life." If your mind is set in regard to your prayer—that is, if you are convinced that He will do what He has promised you, if you are pure both in what you believe and in what you do—then you will see Him manifested. In this sense, holiness is the key both to being persistent in prayer and to receiving answers to prayer. Holiness is being convinced that what God says and what God does are the same.

You can pray all you want, but you have to be holy to see the answer. Scripture says,

> *If any of you lacks wisdom, he should ask God, who gives generously to all without finding fault, and it will be given to him. But when he asks, he must believe and not doubt, because he who doubts is like a wave of the sea, blown and tossed by the wind. That man should not think he will receive anything from the Lord; he is a double-minded man, unstable in all he does.* (James 1:5–8)

This verse is saying that asking isn't enough. You can spend an hour in prayer and still receive nothing. A person who is *"double-minded..., unstable in all he does"* is demonstrating unholiness because there is an inconsistency between what he says and what he actually believes and does. God is saying to us, in effect, "If you ask Me for something and then doubt that I will give it, don't even think you will receive it." God cannot give it if we doubt because He is holy and must remain true to what He has said in His Word.

Holiness isn't some mystical, nebulous, weird, smoky, cloudy presence. It's very practical and real. Holiness means "one"—not the number one, but one in the sense of "complete." Holiness denotes the concept of being integrated. Integrated comes from the same word as integrity. God has integrity because what He says, what He does, and who He is are the same. That's exactly what holiness means.

God always does what He says He is going to do because He is one with Himself. Why is this important to prayer? Unholiness cannot remain in His presence. In the Old Testament, if someone went into God's presence without being holy, he died. God warned the priests, in effect, "Do not come into My presence unless you are holy, because I am holy. If you come without being holy, it will destroy you." Those who died in that way did not die because God likes to kill people. They died because holiness and unholiness cannot exist together. God says, "The pure in heart will see Me." (See Matthew 5:8.) Those who are impure cannot see God.

If you are holy, what you say, believe, and do will be the same.

When we go to God in prayer, we must have the same integrity between what we say and do that He does, because holiness is telling the truth and then living the truth. God says, *"You will seek me and find me when you seek me with all your heart"* (Jer. 29:13). We can't just *say* we are seeking God; we must *really be seeking Him,* if we want to find Him. In other words, we must be single-minded in our desire to find Him. We must say, like Jacob, "God, I'm not going to let You go until I see you." (See Genesis 32:24–30.)

Is that the way you approach God? If you seek God with all your heart, mind, and conscience, if you seek Him with everything that is in you, He promises that you will find Him. If you do not seek Him with all your heart, mind, passion, and attention, then if God shows up, it means He is not being true to His Word—because He has said He will only come if you seek Him with *all* your heart.

If God were not true to His Word, He would be acting in an unholy way. If we couldn't count on God to do what He says He will do, we couldn't trust Him anymore. He has to be true to His Word, even if it means not answering the prayers that we pray half-heartedly and in unbelief. Note that it was when the followers of Jesus were all in one accord—when they were single-minded—that the Holy Spirit was given. (See Acts 2:1 NKJV.)

It is because we know that God is holy that we can believe He will fulfill what He has promised. We can believe we will receive what we ask of Him according to His Word. Yet James said that if we doubt, we are being double-minded. That means that we don't have integrity—we're not holy. Since God is holy, we also have to be holy if we want to receive answers to our prayers.

This is such an important point that I want to emphasize it once more: Double-mindedness is the opposite of holiness and integrity. If you are integrated, then what you say, what you believe, what you do, and how you respond are the same. If you tell God you believe Him, but then act in the opposite way when you are on your job, taking care of your children, or with your friends, then you are not integrated, pure, holy. You are double-minded. *"That man should not think he will receive anything from the Lord"* (James 1:7).

A KINGDOM OF PRIESTS

These truths concerning the nature of our relationship with God give us a context for the principles we are about to look at from Leviticus 16. We need to see that the requirements God gave in the Old Testament are just as valid for us who live under the new covenant. The difference is that they can now be fulfilled in Christ.

The book of Leviticus is named after the Levites, a tribe of Israel. Aaron, a Levite and the brother of Moses, was the first high priest of Israel. Aaron's descendants became the priestly line. When you read the book of Leviticus, you are reading the commandments God gave the priests.

The Levitical priests were intercessors or mediators between God and the people of Israel. They were a select group within the nation who had this calling. However, the Bible teaches that God has given the word *priest* a broader meaning than this, one that has significant implications for prayer.

In Exodus 19, shortly after God had delivered the children of Israel from slavery in Egypt and *before* He instituted the Levitical priesthood, He told Moses, "Go and tell the people, *'You will be for me a **kingdom of priests** and a holy nation'*" (v. 6, emphasis added). Who were going to be priests? The entire nation of people, both male and female—children, teenagers, young adults, middle-aged adults, and the elderly—were all to be priests.

In God's perspective, the priesthood is ultimately not for a special group of people, but for all those who belong to Him. This was true beginning with the creation of man. God's purposes are eternal, and His original plan for mankind, which began with Adam, was inherited by succeeding generations. God confirmed His plan with Abraham, Isaac, and Jacob, and it was the descendents of Jacob who became the nation of Israel.

God wants to win the world through a priesthood of believers.

Israel inherited God's promise to Abraham: *"Abraham will surely become a great and powerful nation, and all nations on earth will be blessed through him"* (Gen. 18:18). This promise corresponds to God's original plan for mankind to exercise dominion authority on the earth. Therefore, when God called the children of Israel *"a kingdom of priests and a holy nation,"* He was reflecting His purposes for mankind from Adam to Abraham to Jacob to the children of Israel and beyond. God's plan is that man be His representative on earth. The first man was created as a priest—one who served as God's intermediary for the earth. All of Adam's descendants were meant to be priests. Why, then, did God institute the Levitical priesthood?

We know that God wanted Adam to spread His will and His nature throughout the earth, to administrate His kingdom by filling the whole world with a single "nation" of Spirit-led people. Adam failed, and the earth became populated with many nations who did not know God. God then chose one of those nations—Israel—out of all the nations to serve as priest before the other nations. Again, all the people of this nation were to be priests. Yet Israel also failed to fulfill God's calling. So God chose a small group from the nation, the tribe called the Levites, to serve as priests. God instructed the Levites to mediate for the nation of Israel. This would enable Israel to fulfill its calling to go to the other nations of the world as God's representative so that, ultimately, all nations would return to Him. That was the purpose of the Levitical priesthood: to restore the purpose of God to Israel.

However, this priesthood also failed to follow God and became corrupted. Then God sent the prophets to tell the priests to return to Him, but Israel killed or ignored the prophets. Therefore, God had to come personally. God raised up a Priest, not only from the line of Abraham but also from His own house, One who would be faithful—Jesus, the second person of the Trinity, the Son of God, our High Priest:

> *No one takes this honor* [of being a priest] *upon himself; he must be called by God, just as Aaron was. So Christ also did not take upon himself the glory of becoming a high priest. But God said to him, "You are my Son; today I have become your Father." And he says in another place, "You are a priest forever, in the order of Melchizedek."* (Heb. 5:4–6)

This Priest didn't fail. He served God perfectly. He knew how to enter God's presence and how to represent man to God and God to man. In doing so, He created a new nation of people who would be God's priests to the world. This nation is called the church. What did God say to the church?

The same thing He had said to Israel. The apostle Peter wrote,

> You also, like living stones, are being built into a spiritual house to be a holy priesthood, offering spiritual sacrifices acceptable to God through Jesus Christ.... But you are a chosen people, a royal priesthood, a holy nation, a people belonging to God, that you may declare the praises of him who called you out of darkness into his wonderful light.   (1 Pet. 2:5, 9)

When God told Abraham that He would create a great nation from Abraham's lineage and that through him all the nations of the world would be blessed, what was His intent? It was to redeem the whole world. In keeping His Word, God created a new nation from Abraham's descendent, Jesus of Nazareth, and his spiritual offspring who believe in Jesus—*"those who are of the **faith** of Abraham"* (Rom. 4:16, emphasis added).

God created a new nation of Spirit-filled intercessors.

> It was not through law that Abraham and his offspring received the promise that he would be heir of the world, but through the righteousness that comes by faith....The promise comes by faith, so that it may be by grace and may be guaranteed to all Abraham's offspring—not only to those who are of the law but also to those who are of the faith of Abraham. He is the father of us all. As it is written: "I have made you a father of many nations." He is our father in the sight of God, in whom he believed.   (vv. 13, 16–17)

This new nation is made up of both Israelites (Jews) and Gentiles (non-Jews) who have placed their faith in Christ. It also breaks down other barriers between people. It is the single nation of Spirit-led people that was God's original purpose: *"There is neither Jew nor Greek, slave nor free, male nor female, for you are all one in Christ Jesus"* (Gal. 3:28). When God chose the Levitical priests, it was a small group, and it was made up only of men. Yet when

God stated in Exodus 19 that the nation of Israel was to be *"a kingdom of priests and a holy nation"* (v. 6), the priesthood included females as well as males. When the people sinned, one of the consequences was that they isolated the priesthood so that it just included males. This is not the case with the spiritual heirs of Abraham. The prophet Joel said:

> *And afterward, I will pour out my Spirit on all people.*
> *Your sons and daughters will prophesy, your old men*
> *will dream dreams, your young men will see visions.*
> *Even on my servants, both men and women, I will*
> *pour out my Spirit in those days.*   (Joel 2:28–29)

This means that when the Lord Himself came to earth as God the Son, His intent was to create a new nation in which everybody would receive the Holy Spirit, through whom they could be God's intermediaries for the world. The idea of women priests was very shocking in the day of Joel. No one had ever heard of a female receiving the anointing of a priest. Yet Joel said, "The time is coming when the sons and daughters will prophesy, the young and the old alike will have the Spirit poured out on them." People were no longer going to be put into categories. If a person repented and received Christ, God would fill that person with His Spirit and make the person His priest.

Therefore, as believers, you and I are priests before God. The Bible calls the priesthood an eternal ordinance. (See Numbers 18:8 NKJV.) It is forever.

TEN STEPS TO PREPAREDNESS IN PRAYER

Aaron, the first high priest, was a type of Christ—who became our High Priest in salvation. Yet Aaron was also a model of the spiritual nation of priests who would serve God in Christ. There is much we can learn from God's instructions to Aaron that will help us understand our New Testament role as *"a royal priesthood"* (1 Pet. 2:9). We can learn how God told Aaron to enter into His presence on the Day of Atonement so we may understand how He wants us to come into His presence today. Here are ten ways we are to prepare to enter the presence of God so we will be able to commune with Him, offer effectual prayer, and be His mediators on behalf of the world.

1. Appropriate God's Grace

First, we need a clear appropriation of God's grace in our lives. Leviticus 16:3 says, *"This is how Aaron is to enter the sanctuary area: with a young bull for a sin offering and a ram for a burnt offering."* Verses five through eleven explain that Aaron was also to take two goats. One was sacrificed as a sin offering for the Israelites. The other was the "scapegoat"—the goat that would represent the taking away of the people's sin by being sent into the desert with the sins of the Israelites on its head.

God instructed Aaron to offer animal sacrifices to make atonement for the sins of Israel. Aaron could not enter the sanctuary area without the sin offering and burnt offering. Similarly, God says to us, "If you desire to enter My presence, your sin has to be dealt with." Therefore, the first subject of prayer is not our list of petitions. Instead, we need to ask ourselves, "Am I in a position to approach God in holiness? Have I examined my own life? Have I explored the possibility that I have thought, said, or been involved in things that are contrary to His Word and His law of love?"

God wants to bless us and answer our prayers. That is why He tells us to repent of sin.

These will not always be glaringly obvious sins. Sometimes they will be more subtle ones. We don't always consider the manner in which we are living our lives before God. For example, the Bible says, *"Let us not give up meeting together, as some are in the habit of doing"* (Heb. 10:25). That's a command. Suppose you say, "I don't feel like going to church today," and you stay home without a good reason for doing so. When you go to God in prayer, God says, in essence, "I have a problem with this. On the one hand, you're trying to get Me to cooperate with you, but on the other hand, you have disobeyed Me. If I answer your prayer,

I am condoning disobedience." This is a matter of God's integrity.

Let's consider another example. I think it's difficult for God to answer our prayers for financial blessing when we aren't tithing. On the one hand, we are robbing God of what is His due (see Malachi 3:8–10), and on the other, we are saying, "Lord, pay my mortgage." When we don't receive the money, we say—unfairly—as the Israelites did, *"Where is the God of justice?"* (Mal. 2:17). This causes God to say to us, in effect, "Now you're trying to put Me in a dilemma. How can I bless you in this when you have disobeyed Me? You're trying to get Me to treat you as if you are holy when, in reality, you are not."

God wants to bless us and answer our prayers. That is why He tells us to deal with our sins. We need to understand and accept Christ's sacrifice for our sins and repent from wrongdoing. We need to make clean the secret closets of sin and disobedience within us so we can be effective in prayer. We are forgiven of our sins when we go to Christ. He covers us with His blood, and we are cleansed. The Scripture says, in 1 John 1:9, *"If we confess our sins, he is faithful and just and will forgive us our sins and purify us from all unrighteousness."* This truth was written to Christian believers who already had a relationship with Christ. We need to be cleansed continually so we can live before God in holiness— the holiness Christ died to provide for us.

God is essentially saying to us, "If you want Me to do business with you, you have to get rid of sin, disobedience, and neglect." *"But your iniquities have separated you from your God; your sins have hidden his face from you, so that he will not hear"* (Isa. 59:2). The point is not to go around feeling guilty about these sins, but rather to ask for forgiveness and be cleansed. God is gracious to us. We can even ask Him to forgive us for sins we don't realize we're committing. King David prayed, *"Who can discern his errors? Forgive my hidden faults"* (Ps. 19:12). We also have this promise from God's Word:

For as high as the heavens are above the earth, so great is his love for those who fear him; as far as the

*east is from the west, so far has he removed our
transgressions from us.* (Ps. 103:11–12)

How do we receive forgiveness? We don't bring animal
sacrifices as the Israelites needed to, but we still must have
our sins atoned for by blood. The *principles* of the Old Testament are still in effect in the New. Yet the New Testament
reveals their deepest application and significance. For example, *"the* [Old Testament] *law requires that nearly everything be cleansed with blood, and without the shedding of
blood there is no forgiveness"* (Heb. 9:22). The difference is
that the sacrifice was fulfilled once and for all in Christ, the
Lamb of God. *"He sacrificed for their sins once for all when
he offered himself"* (Heb. 7:27).

1 John 1:7 says,

*The blood of Jesus, his Son, purifies us from all sin. If
we walk in the light, as he is in the light, we have
fellowship with one another.*

This verse is talking about relationship. When you are
cleansed with the blood of Jesus, everything is all right because there's nothing between you and God. He knows
you're clean. When your sins are forgiven and you are right
with God, you can genuinely fellowship with Him and with
other believers—and that brings the power of agreement in
prayer.

God is serious about holiness and obedience. We can't
live in sin and unbelief if we want our prayers answered. If
you're struggling with a particular sin, surrender it to God,
ask Him to purify you from it (1 John 1:9), and seek the
counsel of mature believers so that it will not block your
relationship with God.

2. Put on Righteousness

The second preparation is found in Leviticus 16:4. I call
it "putting on righteousness." This step corresponds to the
New Testament admonition, *"Put on the new self, created to
be like God in true righteousness and holiness"* (Eph. 4:24).

Leviticus 16:4 explains how Aaron was to enter God's holy place:

> *He is to put on the sacred linen tunic, with linen undergarments next to his body; he is to tie the linen sash around him and put on the linen turban. These are sacred garments; so he must bathe himself with water before he puts them on.*

The priest was to wear the right clothes—the clothes God said to wear. The priest had his own clothing, but God said, in effect, "If you want to come into My presence, clothe yourself with what I tell you to put on." The application for us comes from Ephesians 6:11–20, in which Paul talked about putting on the *"full armor of God"* (vv. 11, 13). I believe this analogy is misunderstood. It is not so much a military concept as a preparatory one. It is talking about preparing for prayer (vv. 18–20). Before you pray, you need to be wearing *"the helmet of salvation"* (v. 17). This refers to atonement: being saved and having the blood of Christ applied to your sins. You are also to put on *"the breastplate of righteousness"* (v. 14). This means being right with God through the righteousness of Christ.

We come into God's presence only through the righteousness of Christ.

Why was the priest to wear linen? Linen is a fabric that breathes; there was to be no perspiration in God's presence. Why? It is because sweat represents rebellion against God.

> *To Adam [God]* said, *"Because you listened to your wife and ate from the tree about which I commanded you, 'You must not eat of it,' cursed is the ground because of you; through painful toil you will eat of it all the days of your life. It will produce thorns and thistles for you, and you will eat the plants of the field. By the sweat of your brow you will eat your food."*
> (Gen. 3:17–19)

Sweating over work was not in God's original plan. It is a result of Adam's disobedience.

Let's look at the broader meaning of this idea. Sweat represents any attempt to reach God on our own merits. It means trying to work ourselves into God's presence. Do we see examples of this today? Suppose a person's heart isn't right before God. To compensate, he sends three hundred dollars to the Red Cross. In itself, there's nothing wrong with a gift to the Red Cross. Yet God says, in effect, "That's not going to get you into My presence. You're sweating. You're trying to get Me to like you by doing good deeds, while at the same time you're living contrary to My Word." That's sweating. Instead, we are to put on the breastplate of righteousness. A breastplate protects the heart and other precious organs. With this analogy, God is saying, "I want you to be pure in the most vital areas of your life." We can do that only by appropriating the righteousness of Christ through faith: *"God made him who had no sin to be sin for us, so that in him we might become the righteousness of God"* (2 Cor. 5:21). Then we need to live in that righteousness, doing what is right by keeping in step with the Spirit. (See Galatians 5:25.)

When we put on God's righteousness, we can rejoice before the Lord:

> *I delight greatly in the LORD; my soul rejoices in my God. For he has clothed me with garments of salvation and arrayed me in a robe of righteousness, as a bridegroom adorns his head like a priest, and as a bride adorns herself with her jewels.* (Isa. 61:10)

3. Put On Truth and Honesty

The next preparation is truth and honesty. Let us look again at Leviticus 16:4: *"He is to tie the linen sash around him."* We need the sash as well as the breastplate. The sash covers the most delicate areas of your life, the parts you don't like to talk about, the secret life only you know about. David said, *"Surely you desire truth in the inner parts; you teach me wisdom in the inmost place"* (Ps. 51:6).

Do we fear the Lord, so that we desire to be people of truth? Ephesians 6:14 says, *"Stand therefore, having your loins girt about with truth"* (KJV). We are to be girded with the sash of truth so that we are transparent and clean before the Lord. Is this your desire? There isn't any difference between the preparation of the high priest in the Old Testament and what God wants of us now. *"Who may ascend the hill of the LORD? Who may stand in his holy place? He who has clean hands and a pure heart"* (Ps. 24:3–4). We need to be pure before God by turning from our sinful ways, receiving forgiveness through Christ, and walking in the Spirit. (See Romans 8:3–4.)

4. Cleanse with the Word

"These are sacred garments; so he must bathe himself with water before he puts them on" (Lev. 16:4). Before we can enter God's presence, we must be cleansed. In John 15:3, Christ said to His disciples, *"You are already clean because of the word I have spoken to you."* He also prayed to the Father, *"Sanctify them by the truth; your word is truth"* (John 17:17). Ephesians 5:25–26 says, *"Christ loved the church and gave himself up for her to make her holy, cleansing her by the washing with water through the word."*

God doesn't want us to think that singing hymns in a worship service is sufficient for entering His presence. Christ said we are clean through the words He has spoken. What cleanses us? The Word of God. This is why we need to continually meditate on the Scriptures.

In the Old Testament, Aaron had to cleanse with actual water. He had to wash his entire body and put on linen so that, when he went into the holiest places of the tabernacle, he would be clean. With the fulfillment of the law in the New Testament, we no longer have to wash with actual water. The Word of God is our water for spiritual cleansing. David emphasized this truth:

> *How can a young man keep his way pure? By living according to your word. I seek you with all my heart; do not let me stray from your commands. I have hidden your word in my heart that I might not sin against you.* (Ps. 119:9–11)

You need to make sure you are in the Word when you come before God—that you've *read* the Word, that the Word is *in* you, that you are *obeying* the Word. Otherwise, you will enter God's presence with your own ideas and attitudes. However, the Word will wash you so completely that it will change your heart and mind, even without your realizing it. In addition, things that you might not have thought were important, but were important to God, will be transformed within you. For example, it is easy for us to forget the command, *"Do not lie to each other, since you have taken off your old self with its practices"* (Col. 3:9). We tell little lies. We tell people we will meet them at a certain time. When we arrive late, we're embarrassed, so we tell a lie about why we were late. In a variety of ways, we cover up for ourselves, trying to protect our reputations. The Word will purify our attitudes and actions.

> **The cleansing of the Word will change your heart and mind and transform your life.**

You become what you listen to. You become what you think. You become what's in your mind. If your mind is filled with the Word of God, then you will start becoming what it says. It will wash you.

5. Worship and Praise God

> [Aaron] *is to take a censer full of burning coals from the altar before the LORD and two handfuls of finely ground fragrant incense and take them behind the curtain. He is to put the incense on the fire before the LORD, and the smoke of the incense will conceal the atonement cover above the Testimony, so that he will not die.* (Lev. 16:12–13)

In the Bible, incense is the symbol of worship. God is saying that when your sins are covered and your heart is pure, when you are being honest and your motives are right, and when you are being cleansed by the Word, then it is time to worship. Jesus said to the woman at the well, in effect, "The Samaritans are trying to find God on the mountain. The Jews are trying to find God in the temple in

Jerusalem. Yet if you really want to come into God's presence, you must worship God in spirit and in honest motivation—in truth. That is when you truly worship." (See John 4:19–24.)

If you wanted something from somebody, and that person told you that if you did a, b, and c, you would receive it, what would you do? You would do a, b, and c, depending on how badly you wanted it. God says that in order to come into His presence, we need to worship. He has told us what to do, but sometimes we try to bypass this step and get right into prayer. God is saying to us, "Honor My name first. Worship Me." He wants us to put some incense on the fire.

This is why worship leaders are so important in the body of Christ. They are the ones who prepare the way for the congregation to come into the presence of the Lord. Therefore, if the worship leaders' hearts aren't right, there can be problems. If our corporate worship is not what it's supposed to be, our worship leaders need to examine their hearts. Are they putting incense on the fire, or are they jumping over the fire trying to get into God's presence without paying the price of purity? The same thing is true for you and me. We're priests before God. We have to make sure we are able to worship.

6. Separate Yourself

No one is to be in the Tent of Meeting from the time Aaron goes in to make atonement in the Most Holy Place until he comes out, having made atonement for himself, his household and the whole community of Israel. (Lev. 16:17)

We prepare for prayer by separating ourselves from our normal environment, our normal activities. When you are seeking God, you can't be listening to the radio or watching television. You can't be listening to other people talking. You can't be around distractions. If you're going to seek God, you have to be serious about it. God says, "If you want to find Me, you will do so only if you seek Me with all your heart." (See Jeremiah 29:13.)

God didn't meet Aaron anywhere and everywhere. Aaron was to go into the Tent of Meeting. God said, "That is where I meet—in the Tent." To enter the Tent, Aaron had to have certain things right. Aaron's two sons tried to do things their own way. God said, "No, they haven't met the requirements of meeting Me here." (See Leviticus 9:23–24; 10:1–2.)

As with Aaron, God doesn't meet you just anywhere and in any way. There is a place in God in which He meets you. In the Old Testament, there was an actual tent, a physical place. Yet the New Testament fulfills the Old Testament. This means that there is still a place where God meets you in prayer, but it's not a building. It's not even your body. It's a place *in God*. God has prepared a place in Him just for you, and you need to enter that place. If your heart, your attitude, or your motives aren't right—if there are things in your life that aren't right—God says, "You aren't yet in the place where I want you to be."

One way to reach this place is by fasting, a topic that we will explore later. When you fast, you eliminate distractions. You remove yourself from many things that have been clogging up your life and disturbing your spirit. You will feel freer, less encumbered. You will have more time. Then you will be on your way to that place in God. How soon you reach it can depend on how fast you want to move, how deep you want to get, how quickly you want to be cleansed, how honest you want to be, how serious and sincere you are. Yet when you do make it to that place in God, everybody will know it because you will be sparkling. Isaiah 58 says that if you fast correctly, then *"your light will break forth like the dawn"* (v. 8).

7. Believe

Next, we need to have faith in God's power to do what He has promised.

Then [Aaron] *shall come out to the altar that is before the* LORD *and make atonement for it. He shall take some of the bull's blood and some of the goat's blood*

83

*and put it on all the horns of the altar. He shall sprin-
kle some of the blood on it with his finger seven times
to cleanse it and to consecrate it from the uncleanness
of the Israelites.*   (Lev. 16:18–19)

In the Old Testament, there was atoning power through the animal sacrifices. Yet the priest had **God wants us to believe His power can accomplish what He has promised.** to believe that, when he put the blood on the horns of the altar, God's power was great enough to atone for sin. He had to have faith. The people also had to believe. After the sacrifices were offered on their behalf and the scapegoat sent out into the desert, they had to go back to their homes saying, "My sins are forgiven for another year." They had to believe that the power manifested in the offering of the sacrifices forgave their sins.

In the Hebrew culture, the horn represented power. This means that every time the high priest entered the Holy Place, he had to deal with God's power. To do this, he needed to be prepared to enter. His life had to be right. Likewise, God's power will be manifested when your life is right. When you feel spiritually dry, when you're not experiencing God's power, examine your life. Check to see if you are right with God.

In requiring the high priest to sprinkle blood on the horns of the altar, I believe God was telling us, "I want you to confess that I have power to do anything I have promised you." The mixed blood of bulls and goats didn't have any power in itself. Yet when the priest put the blood on the horns of the altar, it had power to atone for the sins of Israel. Thank God for His power!

When did the cleansing and consecration of the altar from the uncleanness of the people take place? At the seventh time the blood was sprinkled on the horns of the altar. (See verse 19.) Seven is the number of perfection, and the perfection of forgiveness and sanctification was manifested with the coming of Christ. After Christ died on the cross, the animal sacrifices were done away with because He had sacrificed Himself once for all people and for all time: *"Unlike the other high priests, he does not need to offer sacrifices day after day, first for his own sins, and then for the sins of the people. He sacrificed for their sins once for all when he offered himself"* (Heb. 7:27). *"God presented him as a sacrifice of atonement, through faith in his blood"* (Rom. 3:25).

How can the blood of a Man who died two thousand years ago cleanse me today? I wasn't around when Adam sinned. I wasn't there when Jesus died. How in the world can His blood forgive my sins in the twenty-first century? It is because the blood still has power. God says to us, in effect, "Listen to Me. I received the animal sacrifices that the high priests brought to Me. When My power connected with them, it was so potent that it atoned for the sins of three million Israelites. How much more will the *'precious blood of Christ, a lamb without blemish or defect'* (1 Pet. 1:18)—the blood of My own Son—atone for your sins?"

God can forgive you two thousand years later because Jesus went to the Holy of Holies in heaven.

> *When Christ came as high priest of the good things that are already here, he went through the greater and more perfect tabernacle that is not man-made, that is to say, not a part of this creation. He did not enter by means of the blood of goats and calves; but he entered the Most Holy Place once for all by his own blood, having obtained eternal redemption. The blood of goats and bulls and the ashes of a heifer sprinkled on those who are ceremonially unclean sanctify them so that they are outwardly clean. How much more, then, will the blood of Christ, who through the eternal Spirit offered himself unblemished to God, cleanse our consciences from acts that lead to death, so that we may serve the living God!* (Heb. 9:11–14)

Christ is the atoning Sacrifice for the sins of the whole world. (See 1 John 2:2.) His blood is worthy. He had to be slain only once. In the Old Testament, the power of the blood lasted for just one year. The high priest had to come back the next year on the Day of Atonement and sacrifice again. I thank God that when John saw Jesus coming to the Jordan River to be baptized, he said, "Look—God has provided His own Lamb." (See John 1:29.) John didn't say Jesus is the lamb of man. He said Jesus is the Lamb of God. God Himself provided this Lamb as the Sacrifice for our sins. That is why we can enter boldly into the Holy of Holies where God dwells (Heb. 4:16 NKJV)—trembling because we fear God, but confident because we know the blood of Jesus has cleansed us. We must believe in the effectiveness of His sacrifice on our behalf.

8. Give God the Glory

Leviticus 16:25 says, "[Aaron] *shall also burn the fat of the sin offering on the altar."* After we enter God's presence through the blood of Jesus, believing in His power to cleanse us, we are to give God the glory.

When God gave instructions about sacrificing, He told the Israelites to collect the fat of the sacrifices. He told them not to eat the fat, but to place it on the altar and burn it to Him. Fat is a symbol of glory because fat is excess. God is saying, "I don't want you to take any glory for yourself for this forgiveness and atonement. I want all the fat to be given to Me. I want you to confess that I am the One who accomplished this. I want you to give Me all the glory for it." In giving God the glory, we can say, "Thank you, God, for receiving me, forgiving me, cleansing me, redeeming me, and making me fit to be in Your presence where Your glory is."

God deserves all the glory because He has given us both life and redemption: *"I am the LORD; that is my name! I will not give my glory to another or my praise to idols"* (Isa. 42:8). *"How can I let myself be defamed? I will not yield my glory to another"* (Isa. 48:11).

God loves glory. He loves the excess. When God blesses us and we can't use all that we've been given, that's fat, that's glory. God says to us, "You have excess. You have glory in your house. Offer it to Me." Our response should be, "I have some glory, some extra money and goods. I want to give them to God so that someone else who needs them can also be blessed."

What are you doing with your excess?

9. Wash in the Word

You may ask, "Why do we need to wash in the Word again? We are already being cleansed through it." The first use of the Word is for cleansing. The second is for appropriating God's promises.

Leviticus 16:26 says, *"The man who releases the goat as a scapegoat must wash his clothes and bathe himself with water; afterward, he may come into the camp."* I believe that God is saying through this verse, "You have done all that you are supposed to do, and you have given Me the glory. I am pleased. Go ahead and tell Me what you want." Since everything is clear between you and God, you can now *"present your requests to God"* (Phil. 4:6). Wash yourself in the Word by asking God to fulfill His purposes based on His will and promises.

10. Remain in the Anointing

Finally, we need to remain in the anointing—in a right relationship with God—so we may continually dwell in our meeting place with God. We must remember to follow His instructions and ways if we want to remain in His presence.

> *The priest who is anointed and ordained to succeed his father as high priest is to make atonement. He is to put on the sacred linen garments and make atonement for the Most Holy Place, for the Tent of Meeting and the altar, and for the priests and all the people of the community.* ***This is to be a lasting ordinance for you*** *[My people].* (Lev. 16:32–34, emphasis added)

We can live in a continual state of union with God because of Christ's atonement for our sins. When Jesus Christ came, He was anointed and ordained as High Priest by God, and His atonement is fulfilled and sustained for all time. All the high priests who came before Him were only types of Him. The atonement that He made is eternal; therefore it remains an everlasting ordinance. *"When this priest had offered for all time one sacrifice for sins, he sat down at the right hand of God"* (Heb. 10:12).

To be able to enter God's presence, we have to remain in this state of preparedness for prayer. We aren't to approach God in an offhand or careless way. Aaron's sons actually lost their lives when they tried to enter God's presence on their own terms. God is a God of holiness. It is important that we learn what it means to honor the Lord and reflect His nature and character in our lives. These steps of preparation for prayer are important to God because Jesus Christ came to make them all possible. It is because of Christ alone that we can enter the presence of an almighty and holy God and call Him *"Abba, Father"* (Rom. 8:15).

We must follow God's instructions and ways if we want to remain in His presence.

How to Enter God's Presence

LET'S PRAY TOGETHER

Heavenly Father,

Your Word says, *"Blessed are the pure in heart, for they will see God"* (Matt. 5:8). We want to enter into Your presence. We want to be in the place where You meet us. Guide us to that place. Forgive us for being careless and unthinking in the way we approach You. We acknowledge that You are a holy and righteous God. We receive the cleansing of our sins through the blood of Jesus. We worship You in humility and love. Thank you for the privilege of being able to enter with confidence into the place where You dwell, because of the atonement that Your Son has made on our behalf. We pray this in the name of Jesus, the Lamb of God who takes away all our sin. Amen.

PUTTING PRAYER INTO PRACTICE

Ask yourself:

- In what attitude or manner do I approach God in prayer?
- Am I being casual about the sin in my life, without regard for God's holiness?
- Do I think I can get God to hear my prayers by doing good deeds—or do I come to Him through Christ alone?
- What does it mean that I am a member of the priesthood of believers?

Action Steps:

- Before you pray, review the ten steps of preparedness for entering God's presence. See what steps you may be omitting and which areas you need to set right before God.
- Consider your role as priest, or intercessor, before God on behalf of the world. Let that knowledge guide how you pray.

Principles

1. As believers, we are *"a chosen people, a royal priesthood, a holy nation, a people belonging to God"* (1 Pet. 2:9).
2. As God's priests, we are to intercede for others so they will return to God and be coworkers in His purposes.
3. Ten steps of preparedness for entering God's presence in prayer are:
   - *Appropriate God's Grace:* Acknowledge God's holiness, turn away from your sins, and be cleansed through the blood of Christ.
   - *Put on Righteousness:* Appropriate the righteousness of Christ through faith. Live in that righteousness, doing what is right by keeping in step with the Spirit.
   - *Put On Truth and Honesty:* Be transparent and clean before the Lord, desiring truth in the innermost parts and living with integrity.
   - *Cleanse Yourself with the Word:* Before you come before God, make sure that you've *read* the Word, that the Word is *in* you, and that you are *obeying* the Word.
   - *Worship and Praise God:* Honor and worship God in spirit and in truth (John 4:24–24), acknowledging Him as your All in All.
   - *Separate Yourself:* Remove yourself from your normal environment, activities, and distractions. Find the place in God where He meets you by coming to Him with the right heart, attitude, and motives.
   - *Believe:* Have faith in God's power to do what He has promised and in the effectiveness of Christ's sacrifice.
   - *Give God the Glory:* Confess that God is the One who accomplished your atonement, forgiveness, and reconciliation with Him, and is worthy to be praised. Give to others out of the abundance God has given you.
   - *Wash in the Word:* Ask God to fulfill His purposes based on His will and the promises in His Word.
   - *Remain in the Anointing:* Remain in a state of preparedness for prayer. Honor the Lord by reflecting His nature and character in your life.

Chapter Five

Cultivating the God Kind of Faith

There is positive faith and there is negative faith. Both come by the same means—by what we listen to and believe.

In the previous chapter, we learned what it means to prepare our hearts to enter God's presence so we can eliminate obstacles to unanswered prayer and be effective in God's purposes. In this chapter, I want to examine another reason why our prayers may fail to work. It may be because we often have the wrong kind of faith. I didn't say that we *lack* faith. I said we have the wrong *kind* of faith. Understanding the different kinds of faith, and how faith functions, are key preparations for prayer.

EVERYONE LIVES BY FAITH

Every day, you and I live by faith. In fact, everyone lives by faith. When we read in the Bible, *"The just shall live by faith"* (Rom. 1:17 NKJV; Gal. 3:11 NKJV), we have to define what the Bible means by this statement, because faith of some kind is working in our lives, whether we are aware of it or not.

If we are going to do any kind of business with God, we need to be able to function in the faith the Bible speaks of. *"Without faith it is impossible to please God"* (Heb. 11:6). Many of us were taught that faith is necessary. However, we usually weren't taught how to obtain the faith that is pleasing to God.

WHAT IS FAITH?

First, how do we define faith in general terms? The New Testament word *"faith"* comes from the Greek word *pistis*, which simply means "belief" or "confidence." Having faith means believing and having confidence in the words that you hear. It is believing in something that is not seen as though it is already a reality—and then speaking it and expecting it until it manifests itself. Everyone lives by this definition of faith, and people usually receive exactly what they have faith for. Why? Men and women were created in God's image to operate in the same way He does— through words of faith. *"For he spoke, and it came to be; he commanded, and it stood firm"* (Ps. 33:9).

> **We were created to operate in the way God does—through words of faith.**

God created by believing in the reality of what He would create before He saw its manifestation. *"By faith we understand that the universe was formed at God's command, so that what is seen was not made out of what was visible"* (Heb. 11:3). God not only spoke words to create things, but He even uses words to keep the universe running. Hebrews 1:3 says, *"The Son is the radiance of God's glory and the exact representation of his being, sustaining all things by his powerful word."* God sustains everything by the power of His Word. He spoke, and the universe came into being. He keeps on speaking, and this keeps the universe going. The principle is this: When you ask for something in prayer, you have to start speaking about it as if it already exists. Moreover, you have to *keep* on speaking in order to see its manifestation. Then, when it comes, it is not enough to receive it from God. You have to be able to keep what God has blessed you with. How do you keep it? By speaking it. When the devil tries to steal it, you are to say, "No, faith brought this to me; faith keeps it mine; this belongs to me."

This is why, when you lose anything to the locusts (see Joel 2:25–26), you can still get it back. When you receive something from God according to His promise, you obtain the title deed to it. If Satan steals what you have received from God, who has the title deed? You do. That means you still own the property even though he has possession of it.

Think about something that you know you received from God but have since lost. You can appropriate the promise that says everything the locust has eaten, God will restore. Then you can use your faith to start expecting it. Every time you speak of it, it will get closer. And when it comes back, it will come back multiplied, in some form or another. The devil loses out if he steals what God has given us because God will multiply it back to us. If you expect what God has promised, it will come. If you don't expect it, it will not come.

THE WORD OF FAITH

In Romans, we read, *"But the righteousness that is by faith says:...'The word is near you; it is in your mouth and in your heart'"* (Rom. 10:6, 8). What is this passage referring to? *"The word of faith"* (v. 8). Where is it? It *"is near you; it is in your mouth and in your heart."* I think the word *"near"* has to do with what you are listening to. When you turn on the television, words of faith—that is, words that create the raw material for your belief—are near you. The same thing is true when people talk to you. This means that the person sitting next to you is very influential. What he or she says to you goes into your ears. Your ears are the gateway to your heart, and *"out of the overflow of the heart the mouth speaks"* (Matt. 12:34). What you say is a reflection of what is in your heart, of what you believe. You will likely have what you say because God has given you the same ability He possesses—creative expression through your words. Just as God created His world with His words, so you create your world with your words. Again, every word is a word of faith. Therefore—

Faith is belief in action.

In fact, *faith is the greatest element in advanced civilization.* What do I mean by this? Human faith has given birth to great achievement, and still does. Nothing in the world is more powerful than belief. All the people in the world who have ever dealt with human development agree with this fact. Why? Because belief creates your life, and that's what faith is: believing things that you haven't yet seen to the point that you act on them until they come into being. It is through faith that people experience personal growth and success.

This is a crucial truth for us to remember. *Faith is active belief. It is belief combined with expectation and action.* Have you ever expected to fail and then failed? That's faith. You expect you are not going to get a loan, and so you talk yourself out of it on the way to the bank. You tell yourself all the reasons why you can't get it; you preach this to yourself, so that you say, "There's no use in my going, but let me try it anyway." When you don't get it, you confirm your belief by saying, "Just as I expected."

I believe that sometimes God doesn't answer our prayers because He understands how powerful the principle of faith is and knows that what we're asking for wouldn't be good for us. Perhaps you have been asking God to speak to you for a long time. Many of us have prayed this way: "Oh, God, speak to me. Tell me this, tell me that, and direct me in this." "Oh, Lord, I don't hear Your voice anymore. You don't speak to me." We are passionate about wanting God to speak to us. The book of James says that the righteous man is *"quick to listen, slow to speak"* (James 1:19). In other words, we can talk too much about the wrong thing. God doesn't answer us because He doesn't want us to have what is not right for us. God wants us to talk to Him. However, He wants us to pray in a way that reflects the faith that He gives because such prayer is based on His good purposes for us.

"HAVE THE GOD KIND OF FAITH"

We've just discussed the overall principle of how faith works. However, I want you to notice the qualification Paul gave in Romans 10. He said, *"The word is near you; it is in* *your mouth and in your heart,' **that is, the word of faith we are proclaiming**"* (Rom. 10:8, emphasis added). Paul said that the word of faith he wanted to plant in believers' hearts was the one he was preaching, the one given by God.

One of the most important illustrations in the Bible concerning faith and prayer is found in Mark:

> *The next day as they were leaving Bethany, Jesus was hungry. Seeing in the distance a fig tree in leaf, he went to find out if it had any fruit. When he reached it, he found nothing but leaves, because it was not the season for figs. Then he said to the tree, "May no one ever eat fruit from you again." And his disciples heard him say it.* (Mark 11:12–14)

What did Jesus do? He used words. What kind of words did He use? Words of faith. Remember that faith is active belief. When He spoke to the tree, He actively believed that the tree would die.

Did you know there is scientific proof of the power of the spoken word? I once saw a National Geographic program on television that described how plants grow. It reported on a study of the difference between speaking positively to plants and speaking negatively to them. In one experiment, people told plants positive things such as, "You are beautiful; you are growing so well." The plants flourished. With a different group of plants, people said, "You are withering; you are ugly," and similar negative words. The plants wilted.

What happened to the tree Jesus spoke to? *"In the morning, as they went along, they saw the fig tree withered from the roots. Peter remembered and said to Jesus, 'Rabbi, look! The fig tree you cursed has withered!'"* (Mark 11:20–21). Most translations give Jesus' reply as, *"Have faith in God"* (v. 22). Yet this is not the way it was written in the original Greek. Its literal translation is, "Have the God kind of faith."

What you hear creates faith for what you are hearing. Then you speak it, and it happens to you. That is why Jesus said that if we want to operate as He does, we have to have the "God kind of faith":

I tell you the truth, if anyone says to this mountain, "Go, throw yourself into the sea," and does not doubt in his heart but believes that what he says will happen, it will be done for him. Therefore I tell you, whatever you ask for in prayer, believe that you have received it, and it will be yours. (Mark 11:23–24)

The Bible says, *"Faith comes by hearing"* (Rom. 10:17 NKJV). Faith doesn't just initially come by hearing. It continues to come by continual hearing. If you listen to good teaching for one hour and then listen to negative talk for two hours, you are going to have faith for the negative. Faith comes from the word that is near you. That is why I'm careful about the company I keep. I want to be around people who speak words that produce *the faith of God,* because this is the kind of faith we are to have.

If you listen to good teaching for one hour and then negative talk for two hours, you are going to have faith for the negative.

We need to be aware continually that there are other kinds of faith all around us besides the God kind of faith. I encourage you to check the company you're keeping; check what you're listening to and to whom you're listening; check the books you read, the music you listen to, the movies and videos you watch, and the church you attend—because you will become what you listen to and speak what you hear. I can almost tell the kind of company a person has been keeping by what he is saying and the way he is acting. He might have previously demonstrated a certain attitude and then suddenly changed. He has been listening to somebody.

GOD'S FAITH COMES BY HIS WORD

How do you obtain the God kind of faith? Remember that Romans 10:8 says, *"The word is near you; it is in your mouth and in your heart."* Again, whatever is in your heart comes out of your mouth. We could define *"heart"* in this instance as the subconscious mind. It's where you store everything you have been listening to. Again, what comes out of your mouth creates your world because you are just like God in the way you function. Whatever you speak has the power to happen.

I want you to remember this truth because it is going to be the biggest test of your faith. What do you say in the midst of trouble? What do you say when there is adversity? What do you say when things are not going the way you want them to go? What you have been listening to will come out of your mouth, because that is what is in your heart. This is why it's so important to have a constant diet of the Word of God, so that it will get down into your heart. It will nourish your heart so that, when you experience troubles, the Word is what will come out of your mouth, and you will create what the Word says.

Paul said the word that is near you is *"the word of faith we are proclaiming: that if you confess with your mouth, 'Jesus is Lord,' and believe in your heart that God raised him from the dead, you will be saved"* (Rom. 10:8–9). How is a person saved? By confessing with the mouth and believing in the heart. Being born again is difficult for some people to understand because they think there has **What effect are your words having on your life?** to be a feeling connected with the supernatural activity of God. In other words, they say, "I prayed this prayer, but I don't feel anything." That is where they are in error. The Bible says that if a person wants to be saved, he needs to believe and speak—not feel.

It is interesting that the Bible tells us what to say in order to be saved. It doesn't leave it up to us. To be saved, a person must say with his mouth, *"Jesus is Lord"* (v. 9). We say, "God, can't I do something more exciting than that? How about having a light shine down from heaven? How about having me fall down and shake or something? Don't tell me to just talk!" Yet God says, "That's how faith works." When you confess with your mouth and believe in your heart, that's when salvation occurs.

I want you to understand this truth, because it is crucial to your life and your prayers. Your salvation came by the confession of your mouth and the belief in your heart.

When you confessed your faith in the Lord Jesus, He actually, in reality, without a doubt, became your Lord. In light of this truth, consider the following: If you are born again by your words, if you can be kept out of hell and go to heaven by your words, if there is that much power in what you say, what effect are the rest of the words you speak having on you? People say things like, "I'm catching hell on earth," and they're probably right. They said it, so the fire was turned up a little bit more. You can be positively or negatively affected by what you say and believe.

How does this principle apply to prayer? What you keep saying the most is what you will receive. If you pray for something, and then you start saying the opposite, you will get what you say.

Let's look more closely at the statement *"Jesus is Lord"* (Rom. 10:9). The word *lord* means "proprietor" or "owner." If we substitute the word *owner* for *"Lord,"* we can say that we are saved by confessing with our mouths, "Jesus is my Owner! He owns all of my life: lock, stock and barrel; body, mind, and spirit; past, present, and future. He owns my body; I can't take my body anywhere I want to any longer. He owns my mind; I can't put just anything I want to into my mind anymore. He owns my spirit; there's no room for the devil there. He owns my car; I can't use it to do anything negative or evil. He owns my house; I can't do anything immoral in it." In other words, if He is truly your Lord, then it will show up in your attitudes and actions.

We read in 1 Corinthians:

You know that when you were pagans, somehow or other you were influenced and led astray to mute idols. Therefore I tell you that no one who is speaking by the Spirit of God says, "Jesus be cursed," and no one can say, "Jesus is Lord," except by the Holy Spirit. (1 Cor. 12:1–3)

Let's connect the above passage to Romans 10. You are saved by confessing, *"Jesus is Lord,"* and you cannot say this unless the Holy Spirit enables you. You cannot fake this confession—saying that Jesus is your Lord and then doing only what you feel like doing. If you say that Jesus is your Lord, but you aren't living as if He owns your life, you are insulting Him. You probably know people who say they are believers, who claim they have accepted Christ as Lord, but whose lifestyle hasn't changed. They are still coveting, gossiping, lying, stealing, drinking, using drugs, or living in adultery, but then they go to church and take communion. They say that Jesus is their Lord, but they are not living by the Spirit of Christ.

When you truly confess and believe, "Jesus is my Lord," all heaven goes into action to make sure you receive the Holy Spirit because heaven recognizes the word of faith. After you make your confession, it needs to remain a reality in your life. You need to continue affirming, "Jesus is my Lord." God knows if you are serious about your confession because only the Holy Spirit can confirm it.

"For it is with your heart that you believe and are justified, and it is with your mouth that you confess and are saved. As the Scripture says, 'Anyone who trusts in him will never be put to shame'" (Rom. 10:10–11). When you say that Jesus is your Lord, you have to trust that He truly is. If you keep believing that and saying that, the Bible says you will not be made ashamed.

Suppose you tell people, "I have confessed Jesus as my Lord, and I am a child of God." They may say, "Well, how do we know that? You're still the same person we always knew." Yet if you keep confessing and believing it, you will not be made ashamed. They will see the difference in you. They are going to know something has happened. If you keep staying in His Word and doing His Word, He will truly become Lord of all areas of your life.

If you keep confessing and believing, you will not be made ashamed.

I've heard people say that Jesus is Savior, but not Lord, in someone's life. I believe that is impossible. I think this saying is more to the point: "If Jesus is not Lord *of* all, then He's not Lord *at* all." You can't have Him as Savior and not Lord because you wouldn't be reflecting true belief in Him.

PLANTED BY THE WORD

Let's connect this idea to prayer. The same principle applies. If you believe what you pray, if you ask God to make a way for you concerning a situation on your job or a relationship or an idea He's given you for a business, if you confess and hold on to God's truth concerning your situation, you will not be made ashamed. For instance, God has promised that if we live righteously and delight in His Word, we will be *"like a tree planted by streams of water, which yields its fruit in season and whose leaf does not wither,"* and that whatever we do will prosper (Ps. 1:1–3). You can claim that Scripture for yourself: "I am like a fruitful tree, planted by streams of water. My job is like a tree (my relationship is like a tree), planted by rivers of waters. It will bring forth promotion (reconciliation) in season, and everything I do will prosper." If you say that in prayer, and then you keep saying it and believing it, God says, "You won't be made ashamed concerning it."

The first day you claim God's promise, people may start laughing at you and say, "I haven't seen anything change in your life." The third day, they may still laugh at you. Keep saying it and believing it, though. If God has promised it, He wants you to claim it. He says, "You will not be made ashamed." In the end, you are the one who is going to be laughing—with joy.

When you stay connected to the Word of God, you will bear fruit in season.

However, you have to keep believing. This is why, if you are a righteous person living by faith, you have to keep company with the same type of people. It's difficult to start believing and then spend most of your time around people who aren't living in faith, because then you begin to pick up their attitudes, which can kill belief.

The Bible says that Christ washes us by the washing of water, by the Word.

Christ loved the church and gave himself up for her to make her holy, cleansing her by the washing with water through the word, and to present her to himself as

*a radiant church, without stain or wrinkle or any other
blemish, but holy and blameless.*　　　(Eph. 5:25–27)

In the Bible, water is used as a symbol of the Word of
God. The tree mentioned in Psalm 1:3 is *"planted by
streams of water."* It is healthy and yields fruit because it is
near the water and can draw the water by its roots. In the
same way, you have to be connected to the Word of God so
it can flow continuously into your life. Then you will bear
your fruit in its season. You might not see the answer to
your prayer at the moment, but the season is coming because the Word is flowing into your life. Everyone who has
been laughing at your trust in God is going to see your fruit.
Your season is on the way. You can say, "I haven't seen any
results yet, but there's fruit in the tree."

How do you keep believing? You have to be planted.
Plant yourself in a place where the Word is prevalent and
the people around you are continually speaking and living
it. The more time you spend in the Word, the more your
mind is transformed. You begin thinking differently. When
you are constantly around something, when you keep
hearing it, it becomes a part of your heart. You start believing it, and that belief is reflected in what you say. Then
the fruit starts coming.

Some of the things you are praying for right now have
not been manifested because it is not yet their season.
Therefore, between the seed prayer and the manifestation of
the fruit, you have to stay on the riverbank, reading, meditating on, speaking, living, breathing the Word. Plant yourself! In order to keep believing, you have to keep taking in
the Word. In fact, believers need to be riverbanks to each
other. Every time they see each other, they should build
one another up with the Word. One way we can do this is
by *"speak*[ing] *to one another with psalms, hymns and spiritual songs"* (Eph. 5:19). We also have to remind each other
to keep believing, even when the season hasn't yet arrived.

*"'Anyone who trusts in him will never be put to shame.'
For there is no difference between Jew and Gentile—the
same Lord is Lord of all and richly blesses **all** who call on
him"* (Rom. 10:11, emphasis added). God blesses whom?

"All who call on him." Why? It is because of their faith. When you trust in God and believe what He has promised you, God says that He's going to vindicate you in the end. He's going to make you such a blessing that people are going to shake their heads and say, "Tell me about your God." Then you can pass along the word of faith to others.

> *How, then, can they call on the one they have not be-lieved in? And how can they believe in the one of whom they have not heard? And how can they hear without someone preaching to them? And how can they preach unless they are sent?* (Rom. 10:14–15)

Faith is a ministry that God releases. He sends the word of faith, and He uses us to deliver it to others.

LIVING IN REALITY

"So then faith comes by hearing, and hearing by the word of God" (Rom. 10:17 NKJV). Again,

The Word of God needs to be the source we listen to for our faith.

all faith comes by hearing. There is positive faith and there is negative faith, and both come by the same means. *They come by what you listen to and believe.* Faith, active belief, and expectation all come by what we hear. The Word of God needs to be the foremost source we lis-ten to. You can live in a society where everyone else is de-pressed and you are the only one who is happy. It is very possible. Christ did it for thirty-three years. People around Him were depressed, but He was saying things like, *"Be of good cheer."* (See, for example, Matthew 14:27 KJV; Mark 6:50 KJV; John 16:33 KJV.)

Jesus told His disciples to be of good cheer when they were in the midst of a bad storm at sea (Matt. 14:22–33 NKJV). Most people would respond, "You can't be serious. There's nothing to be cheerful about. There's a storm, the boat's breaking apart, the mast is toppling, we're sinking, and you say, *'Be of good cheer'?* You can't see reality, can you?" Does that sound familiar? When you express faith, some people say, "You're not facing reality." We've been trained to think that reality is what we can see. Actually, though, the person who is not living in faith is the one who is not living in reality. *"Faith is being sure of what we hope for and certain of what we do not see"* (Heb. 11:1). Faith is your title deed. A title deed is the evidence or proof of a person's legal ownership. Therefore, faith is the proof of your ownership of what you are praying for.

However, you must make sure you are exercising the God kind of faith. Jesus said, *"If you remain in me and my words remain in you, ask whatever you wish, and it will be given you"* (John 15:7). In effect, He was saying, "Tell Me what I tell you." The God kind of faith puts its full trust in God's Word.

When one of His disciples decided to give Jesus his own opinion, what was Jesus' response?

> *From that time on Jesus began to explain to his disciples that he must go to Jerusalem and suffer many things at the hands of the elders, chief priests and teachers of the law, and that he must be killed and on the third day be raised to life. Peter took him aside and began to rebuke him. "Never, Lord!" he said. "This shall never happen to you!" Jesus turned and said to Peter, "Get behind me, Satan! You are a stumbling block to me; you do not have in mind the things of God, but the things of men."* (Matt. 16:21–23)

Jesus instantly rebuked Peter, telling him that he was not speaking the things of God. What was Jesus hearing? He was hearing Peter say something that contradicted God's will. Therefore, He told Peter, in essence, "Your words are contrary to Mine. You are being a temptation to Me!" Peter was speaking something that was not of God. He was speaking the wrong language. It is interesting to note that Peter later referred to Satan as *"the adversary"* (1 Pet. 5:8). The Greek word for *"adversary"* means "opponent." Satan is the one who speaks the opposite of God's Word. We must be careful not to speak the wrong language by praying for something adverse to God's Word. We also need to be careful not to listen to people who tell us what is contrary

Word or why something can't be done, when God has said it can. Satan's goal is to feed you words contrary to God's words, thereby producing faith for destruction and death.

Keep believing and talking about the goodness of God and the impossibilities that God can bring to pass. The Bible says God fulfills His Word and *"calls things that are not as though they were"* (Rom. 4:17). Affirm in your heart, "This is the beginning of a new lifestyle of faith for me—the God kind of faith." All prayer must be the prayer of faith!

LET'S PRAY TOGETHER

Heavenly Father,
The Bible says, *"'The word is near you; it is in your mouth and in your heart,' that is, the word of faith"* (Rom. 10:8). We pray that we will place our trust in You and Your Word rather than in the words of "faith" all around us that are contrary to Your truth. Forgive us for spending more time dwelling on our own plans, ideas, scenarios, analyses, and schemes than on taking Your Word into our hearts and living by it. Open the truths of Your Word to us and let us rely on You alone. We pray this in the name of Jesus, who is the Living Word. Amen.

PUTTING PRAYER INTO PRACTICE

Ask yourself:

- How much time do I spend in God's Word compared to taking in other perspectives from television, movies, books, magazines, and the Internet?
- Which influences me most—God's Word or what others say?
- If faith is belief in action, what do my actions say about what I believe?
- What negative thoughts and ideas have I allowed to permeate my life?
- Are there people in my life who are more influential on me in a negative way than I am on them in a positive way?

Action Steps:

- List any negative thoughts you think or that others say to you during the day. In the evening, review them and counteract them with what God says in His Word.
- Start developing the God kind of faith by taking one situation in your life and finding out what God's Word says about it. State your findings, pray about the situation in light of them, and hold fast to the Word whenever you are tempted to doubt.
- Decrease the amount of time you spend with negative people, and increase the time you spend with those who are reading and living out the Word. If your spouse and children are negative, live in a way that expresses your own faith and speak the Word of God to them as you have opportunity.
- Challenge: Spend at least as much time in the Word this week as you do watching television.

Principles

1. Unanswered prayer has more to do with our having the wrong *kind* of faith than a *lack* of faith.
2. Men and women were created in God's image to operate in the same way He does—through words of faith.
3. Faith is active belief. It is a point of action or belief combined with expectation.
4. *"The word is near you; it is in your mouth and in your heart"* (Rom. 10:8). There is positive faith and there is negative faith, and both come by the same means. They come by what we listen to and believe.
5. God sometimes doesn't answer our prayers because He understands how powerful the principle of faith is and knows that what we're asking for wouldn't be good for us.
6. What you say is a reflection of what is in your heart—of what you believe. What you keep saying the most is what you will receive.
7. Paul said that the word of faith he wanted to plant in believers' hearts was the one he was preaching—the one given by God. (See Romans 10:8.) This is the faith we are to have.
8. The literal translation of Jesus' statement, *"Have faith in God"* (Mark 11:22) is, "Have the God kind of faith."
9. The God kind of faith comes from hearing His Word.
10. A constant diet of the Word of God will nourish your heart. When you experience troubles, it will be the Word that comes out of your mouth, and you will create what the Word says.
11. If you confess and hold on to God's truth, you will not be made ashamed. He will answer. (See Romans 10:10–11.) When you stay connected to the Word of God, you will bear fruit in season. (See Psalm 1:1–3.)
12. To keep believing, you have to be planted. Plant yourself in a place where the Word is prevalent and the people around you are continually speaking and living it.

Part III

Principles of Prayer

Chapter Six

Jesus' Model Prayer

The secret to Jesus' success in ministry was a lifestyle of prayer.

Of all the things Jesus' disciples observed Him say and do, the Bible records only one thing they asked Him to teach them, and that was how to pray (Luke 11:1). We might wonder, "Why would the disciples ask to learn to pray rather than to do the 'big things' like feeding multitudes, calming storms, casting out demons, healing the sick, raising the dead, or walking on water?" It is because they saw Jesus pray more than anything else.

WHAT THE DISCIPLES OBSERVED

The disciples lived with Jesus. They went everywhere He went and observed Him for three and a half years. Based on the Scriptures, we can deduce that Christ prayed for approximately four to five hours every morning. He also prayed at other times.

For example, the Scripture says, *"Very early in the morning, while it was still dark ["rising up a great while before day" KJV], Jesus got up, left the house and went off to a solitary place, where he prayed"* (Mark 1:35). Jesus would get up while the disciples were still snoring and slip off by Himself behind a bush or a rock and pray there for hours. While they were sleeping, He was praying. Then the disciples would get up and say, "Where's the Master?" When they eventually found Him, they would see Him praying. They saw this every morning. He would spend five hours with God His Father. Then He would say, "Let's go to Jerusalem," or somewhere else, where He would spend two seconds healing a blind man. Notice the ratio: He spent five hours doing one thing and a few seconds doing the other. He continually operated that way. He would spend five hours praying and two minutes casting out a demon or one minute cleansing a leper.

The disciples probably said among themselves, "That's impressive. He cleansed the leper in sixty seconds, but He spent five hours in prayer this morning. This must mean that what He does in the morning is even more important than everything else He does during the day."

The church today hasn't yet understood this truth. We spend a few minutes with God, then we try to do many hours of work in His name. Jesus would cast out a demon with just a word. He'd say, "Come out," and it would leave. It took about two minutes. Yet in the morning, He had spent five hours praying. How do we cast out a demon? We spend five hours working at it, then we say, "Come out." When the demon isn't cast out, we tell someone else to take over. We spend all that time trying to cast out a demon when we've prepared ourselves personally in prayer for only a few minutes that morning.

Martin Luther, one of the greatest Catholic monks in history, started the Reformation that created the Protestant movement and changed the course of the world. Martin Luther said something to the effect of, "When I have a lot to do in a day, I spend more time in prayer, because more work is done by prayer than by work itself." He was right. If I am too busy to pray, I am too busy. If you are too busy to pray, you are too busy.

> "More work is done by prayer than by work itself."
> —Martin Luther

We can never really be too busy to pray because prayer makes our lives much more focused, efficient, and peaceful. Learning this principle has been essential in my life. When I have many things on my heart and mind, a lot of confusion in my life, or overwhelming circumstances to face, I don't try to tackle these problems myself. I go to God in prayer, and He gives me the wisdom and guidance I need to address them.

We often sing, "This is the day that the Lord has made." I imagine God is saying to us, "If this is My day, then why don't you come and talk to Me about it?" We need to ask Him for our day's agenda. We do many things in God's day that He didn't plan for us to do. One hour with God could accomplish ten hours of work because you wouldn't be dealing with trial and error any longer. God would tell you what is really important, compared to what seems urgent. He will tell you what you should do now and what you shouldn't do now. God will supernaturally give you wisdom to address your situation. You will be able to make every act count rather than doing ten things to accomplish one thing. Prayer will enable you to think clearly and wisely. It will give you discernment that you wouldn't otherwise have. Jesus was succinct in His knowledge of what was important because He spent time with the Father. Hours with God makes minutes with men effective.

> **Hours with God make minutes with men effective.**

THE RESULTS OF INTIMACY WITH THE FATHER

In John 5:1–9, we read that Jesus did a great miracle. He healed a man who had been sick for thirty-eight years. The people reacted to this healing; they were deeply impressed. Some were angry. Others wanted answers. Jesus explained something to them that many of us are still trying to grasp. When I discovered the deep truth that Jesus was teaching here, it changed my whole life—my perspective of myself and my relationship to the Father. "*So, because Jesus was doing these things on the Sabbath, the Jews persecuted him. Jesus said to them, 'My Father is always at his work to this very day, and I, too, am working'*" (vv. 16–17). The *New King James Version* reads, "*My Father has been working until now, and I have been working.*"

In effect, Christ was saying to those who questioned His healing, "I spent time with My Father this morning. I already had my whole day worked out for Me because I had fellowship with the One who made days. My Father has already healed the people I'm touching. Their healing is the result of My knowing what My Father is doing. I'm just manifesting it. My Father works; therefore, I work." In essence, what we do should be a manifestation of what God the Father has already done.

What a way to live! "This morning, in prayer, I saw this sick man healed, so I have come to heal him this afternoon." Why? "My Father has already cleansed him. I have come to manifest it."

Look at the next verse. *"For this reason the Jews tried all the harder to kill him; not only was he breaking the Sabbath, but he was even calling God his own Father, making himself equal with God"* (John 5:18). In other words, Jesus was saying that God was His personal, intimate Source. His detractors couldn't take that.

Jesus explained to them how His intimacy with the Father worked.

> *I tell you the truth, the Son can do nothing by himself; he can do only what he sees his Father doing, because whatever the Father does the Son also does. For the Father loves the Son and shows him all he does.* (vv. 19–20)

We spend most of our time during the day trying to figure out what God wants us to do, and we waste the whole day. Christ is saying to us, "I go to the Father first; I see what He's already done, and I do it." This is the pattern He wants us to follow. Remember that prayer is the medium through which man discovers what God has already done in the unseen so that he can give heaven permission through his faith to manifest it on earth. *"Whatever you bind on earth will be bound in heaven, and whatever you loose on earth will be loosed in heaven"* (Matt. 18:18).

When you spend time with God, He reveals what He wants you to do next.

When you spend time with God in the morning, or anytime, He begins to show you what's supposed to be done next. *Prayer saves you time.* Many of us say we believe this principle, but we really don't. We put off praying because we think it is a waste of time, or at least less important than our other activities. We also think the length of time we pray isn't important. Why did Jesus spend hours in prayer? It is because He had a genuine relationship with the Father, and any relationship takes time to build and maintain. God is saying to us, "You will get more done in My presence than you accomplish in the presence of other people. You spend all day talking foolishness with others. They aren't contributing anything to your future. They're just talking. You sit down and spend two or three hours talking politics. In the end, nothing is solved, nothing has changed, and you're depressed. You should have spent those hours on your knees praying for the government, the gangs, and all the other situations." We often discover that when we spend time in prayer, God begins to use *us* to change circumstances.

MANIFESTING THE THOUGHTS OF GOD

Prayer is coming into union with God's mind. God showed Jesus everything He was thinking and said to His Son, "Go and manifest that for Me." There is nothing more intimate than your thoughts. Words are an extension of our thoughts, but we *are* our thoughts. Proverbs 23:7 says, *"As [a man] thinks in his heart, so is he"* (NKJV). God desires not to talk to you, but to "think" to you. This is what Jesus meant when He said, "I do what I see My Father doing" (John 5:19). The text implies, "I do what I mentally see My Father thinking."

A thought is a silent word. A word is a manifested thought. In effect, Jesus was saying, "When I go before God in prayer and spend time with Him, He gives Me His thoughts." Therefore, when Jesus was asked why He healed the sick man, He said, in essence, "I just saw that thought this morning. I am the Word. I manifest the thoughts of God. I have to heal this man because that is what I saw."

"The Son can do nothing by himself; he can do only what he sees his Father doing, because whatever the Father does the Son also does. For the Father loves the Son and shows him all he does" (John 5:19). I recommend that you read the entire book of John. It's a powerful book. Every time Jesus talked about His work, He kept mentioning the love of His Father. You may wonder, "Why does He keep saying that?"

Jesus was saying, in essence, "My Father loves Me so much that He does not just talk to Me, because talking isn't intimate enough. He communes with Me. He loves Me so much that He speaks to My Spirit and mind. The reason I spend time with Him in the morning is to find out what He is thinking, what is on His mind."

Ninety-nine percent of the time God will speak to your mind through your spirit. Many people are waiting for a burning bush or the appearance of an angel. However, they don't hear from God because they're waiting in the wrong way. God doesn't generally speak verbally. That's not intimate enough. He speaks directly to our spirits. For example, you may say, "I think I should bake a cake and take it to Sister So-and-So." That's God. He thought about the cake, and He wanted you to manifest it. God doesn't normally bake cakes. He uses people to bake them for Him. How do you know it is God who is speaking? It is when the idea keeps coming back to you. If you don't bake the cake, two hours later the thought will return. You might dismiss it and then learn that Sister So-and-So needed a cake. Yet you didn't respond to God's prompting because you wanted something more "profound." You wanted a prophet to come to your house and say, "Thus saith the Lord: Bake a cake."

Jesus was naturally supernatural. He would walk up to a man and say, "How long have you been sick?" "Thirty-eight years." "Fine. Take up your bed and walk." Everybody would be fascinated, watching this Man work. He would walk down the street and meet a woman who was bent over. He would say, "Straighten up," and she would straighten up. He would walk a little further and say to someone, "Are you blind?" "Yes." He would touch the person's eyes, and the person would see. The religious people said, "Wait a minute. You're not spiritual enough. You're supposed to say, 'Stand back everybody. I'm getting ready to perform a miracle.'" Religious people spend a long time preparing when they attempt to do miracles. Christ just walked around, spoke, touched—and things happened. People became angry with Jesus because they thought He was not spiritual enough. He was spiritual long before they knew. He was spiritual for five hours so He could be natural for one minute.

Jesus' Model Prayer

HEARING FROM GOD

When you have an important decision to make, pray and fast. If you're trying to decide whether to take a certain job, start a business, go to a specific college, or get married, spend some time with God. God is going to make it easy for you. He helps you avoid making mistakes and doing things twice. Jesus wants us to operate in the way He operated: much time in communion and love with the Father, and much accomplished for the kingdom. Jesus specifically prayed that we would follow His example in this:

That all of them may be one, Father, just as you are in me and I am in you. May they also be in us so that the world may believe that you have sent me. I have given them the glory that you gave me, that they may be one as we are one. (John 17:21–22)

Many people think this verse is talking about unity in the church. Yet Jesus didn't say, "Make them one so *they* can be one." He said, in essence, "Make My disciples one, the way You and I are one with each other. Make them one with You in the same way that I am."

The Father loves you, and He wants the same communion or "common-union" with you that He had with Jesus. Your prayer life can make you so intimate with God that you will walk around and naturally manifest the works, or thoughts, of God, just as Jesus did.

Jesus' detractors said, in effect, "Why did You call God Your Father? Why do you say He speaks to You? That's blasphemy. You cannot be that close to God." (See John 5:16–18.) Let me tell you that God has never appeared to me, but I hear from Him all the time. I have heard God's voice audibly only a few times in my entire life. The rest of His communication to me has been thoughts, ideas, impressions, suggestions in my heart, sensing, and discernment. All of it was God speaking. Jesus' continual reference to "the Father" is critical, because the word *Father* is the Hebrew word *Abba,* which means "source and sustainer." In essence, prayer is the source manifesting its thoughts through the resource.

What are you looking for from God when you pray? Do you want an angel to appear or a prophet to come from a far country to deliver a message from Him? When you love

The Father wants the same communion with you that He had with Jesus. someone, you don't want to receive just a letter; you want to be close to him or her. You want to be intimate with that person. Jesus' relationship with the Father was so intimate that most people didn't know how He spoke with such wisdom and did such miracles. I imagine the people were so impressed that they said to themselves, "He must be doing something we don't know."

The disciples knew Jesus' secret because they observed His lifestyle of prayer. That is why they said, in effect, "Lord, don't teach us to do miracles; teach us to pray." If we learn what they learned, we're going to do the things Jesus did. Let's look now at what Jesus taught His disciples about prayer.

PRAYER DOES NOT COME AUTOMATICALLY

One day Jesus was praying in a certain place. When he finished, one of his disciples said to him, "Lord, teach us to pray, just as John taught his disciples."
(Luke 11:1)

First, the Scripture says, *"One day **Jesus** was praying"* (emphasis added). The disciples were present, but they were not involved. Only Jesus was praying. What were they doing? They were observing Him.

Whenever the Bible mentions Jesus praying, it tells specific things about His actions. For example, it says, *"After he had dismissed them, he went up on a mountainside by himself to pray. When evening came, he was there alone"* (Matt. 14:23). *"One of those days Jesus went out to a mountainside to pray, and spent the night praying to God"* (Luke 6:12). *"Very early in the morning, while it was still dark, Jesus got up, left the house and went off to a solitary place, where he prayed"* (Mark 1:35). Christ never seemed to pray with the disciples. I believe that was intentional on His part.

He wanted them to ask Him about the most important aspect of His ministry. I also believe He prayed alone to teach us that prayer is a personal and private relationship and responsibility. Corporate prayer should never be a substitute for personal and private time with the Father.

Second, the disciples said, *"Lord, teach us to pray."* This implies that prayer was not something they thought they could do without His instruction. As Jewish young men, the disciples had been brought up in the synagogue and the temple, where they had been taught to pray. A part of their daily ritual was to pray in the synagogue, so they were always reading off prayers and repeating prayers. However, Jesus' prayers were different from what they were used to. They saw that there was something distinct about them. They prayed, but He *prayed*. They were busy, but He obtained *results.*

Third, we read in verse two that Jesus began to teach them to pray. He said, *"When you pray...."* This means Jesus agreed that the disciples needed to learn how to pray. He confirmed that prayer is not automatic, but rather a function that must be taught. When a person becomes a believer, he or she is often told, "Read the Word, go to church, and pray." Yet many people don't stop to think that these things don't necessarily come naturally to us. We have to learn how to study the Word, how we are meant to function in the body of Christ, **Contrary to what we've been taught, prayer is not just "talking to God."** and how we are to pray. Again, prayer is not automatic. A new believer may say, "Well, I've never prayed in my life. I do not know how to pray." He or she is often told, "Just talk to God and tell Him how you feel." That sounds good—but that's not what Jesus taught His disciples.

Prayer is not just "talking to God." I used to say that. I used to teach that. I also used to do that, and nothing happened! I had to learn what Jesus taught His disciples before I could become effective in prayer.

If you have difficulty praying, don't feel bad, because many people don't really understand prayer. There are people who make a great amount of noise when they pray. They scream, whoop, holler, groan, and moan. However, that doesn't mean they are praying correctly. Remember that Jesus said, *"And when you pray, do not keep on babbling like pagans, for they think they will be heard because of their many words ["much speaking"* KJV]. *Do not be like them, for your Father knows what you need before you ask him"* (Matt. 6:7–8). There is a lot of *"much speaking"* in many churches and religious groups. However, it is not noise that gets God's attention. It's not how loudly we pray or even the big words we use. There is a way we are to pray, and it has to be learned.

A PATTERN FOR PRAYER

It is very important for us to realize that, regardless of the name it has been given, what Jesus explained to His disciples is not really the "Lord's Prayer." It is a *model* for prayer. In other words, you don't need to repeat the words of this prayer exactly, but should instead use them as a pattern. As we've seen,

> *Prayer is approaching God in order to ask Him to accomplish His will in the earth.*

Christ taught His disciples how to fulfill this purpose. In doing so, He gave them this model to follow:

> *Our Father in heaven, hallowed be Your name. Your kingdom come. Your will be done on earth as it is in heaven. Give us day by day our daily bread. And forgive us our sins, for we also forgive everyone who is indebted to us. And do not lead us into temptation, but deliver us from the evil one.* (Luke 11:2–4 NKJV)

OUR FATHER

*"**Our** Father."* The first thing we learn is that we never bring ourselves to prayer. When we approach God, we are to bring other people's concerns with us. Most of us go to prayer with our own shopping lists: our financial lists, our career lists, and many other things. We say, "Oh, Lord,

please do these things for me." There is selfishness in such a prayer if we don't also pray for others. God will ask, "Where is everybody else? Where is your love and concern for the corporate needs of humanity? All men are my concern." Therefore, we are to begin prayer by thinking of others as well as ourselves. The very first statement of the model excludes most of our prayers, doesn't it?

*"Our **Father**."* Second, we address God as *"Father."* We identify who He is. One definition of the word *father* is "source." We are to go to God with the awareness and confession that He is the Source who can provide for the needs of everyone. Whatever your problem, the Father has the answer. He is *"Abba"* (Mark 14:36), the Source.

IN HEAVEN

*"Our Father **in heaven**."* Next, Jesus is saying, "When you pray, remember that you're not praying to someone on earth." Why? Because that's where the problem is. You need external help. When you say, *"Our Father in heaven,"* you're saying to God, "I recognize that I need help from outside my realm." It is actually a confession of submission. "You're greater than all of us, O Lord. We need external help. We need Your help." In addition, if the Father is not on earth, we need an intermediary. We have to depend on Jesus and the Holy Spirit to be our intermediaries with God. He is in heaven. We are on earth in order to fulfill His plans for the earth.

HALLOWED BE YOUR NAME

"Hallowed be Your name." The word *hallowed* means reverenced, set apart, or sanctified. This means we are to worship the Father as the Holy One. Later on, we can make our requests, but we begin with worship.

When you pray, you are to make God's name holy by honoring all the attributes of His holiness, such as His love, faithfulness, integrity, and grace. You worship. You adore. You exalt. You magnify. You deify. You glorify. After you pray, you continue to honor Him in your life and in all your interactions with others.

How many times have you said, "I don't understand how people can pray for long periods of time. I run out of words to say; I run out of things to pray for"? That's because you haven't known how to pray. Prayer is not giving God a long list of requests. There's so much involved in prayer that you can pray for hours. I can pray for five or six hours nonstop. I've done it. I still do it on occasion. However, if you don't know how to pray, after twenty minutes, you are empty. You are tired and bored, and then you start repeating yourself. Christ says, "Begin by acknowledging that the Father is your All in All, and worship Him." We will never run out of things for which to worship and praise God.

YOUR KINGDOM COME, YOUR WILL BE DONE

"Your kingdom come. Your will be done on earth as it is in heaven." This statement simply means that a true person of prayer is not interested in his own kingdom. His interest is in God's kingdom and what He wants accomplished. We should always ask for the fulfillment of God's prayer list before our own. What a reverse of how we usually do things!

We are to ask, "Father, what do You want done? What do You want to happen on earth?" God is delighted when you are excited about the things He's excited about. He will bless you in the course of accomplishing His work on earth. You don't have to worry about having your needs met if you start praying for God's will to be done on earth in other people's lives.

God will bless you in the course of accomplishing His work on earth.

God likes it when you bring other people's requests to Him and ask Him to meet their needs. Again, that's why you are to pray, *"Our Father."* When you pray for other people, God will bless you because He will see that you have aligned your will with His will, that you are reaching out to others in love and compassion. He is going to answer your own requests because you are obeying Him. He will say, in effect, "I like this person. He isn't selfish. I'm going to make sure his own needs are met."

James 5:16 emphasizes this truth: *"Pray for each other so that you may be healed."* This statement means that when you minister to someone else, God turns around and ministers to what you need. Isn't that just like God? *"Give, and it will be given to you"* (Luke 6:38). Therefore, if you are having problems, find someone else who has problems and start helping him solve his. If you need someone to pray for you, start praying for someone else. If you need financial help, give to someone who has less than you do. Jesus says to us, "Think about God's kingdom first."

GIVE US OUR DAILY BREAD

"Give us day by day our daily bread." With this statement, Jesus is saying, "While you are in God's presence and you are asking Him to be faithful to fulfill His will on earth, include this request." We are to pray, *"Give **us** day by day our daily bread."* The plural tense used in this statement is tied to the *"Our"* in *"Our Father."* If you tell God that you are coming to Him with the concerns of other people, then when you ask for bread, you have to ask for bread for everybody. We normally say, "Lord, provide for me." We're not thinking of anyone else. Yet God tells us once more, "Ask for others as well as yourself. Pray for others."

In Jesus' day, the term "daily bread" was a cultural idiom that referred to everything necessary for the making of bread. Therefore, when you say, *"Give us day by day our daily bread,"* you're not only praying for food, but also for the whole process that is necessary to make the food possible. For example, to make bread, you need sunshine, seed, nitrogen, oxygen, soil, nutrients, minerals, time, growth, development, harvesting, grinding, ingredients to make the bread, mixing, kneading, and baking. Implied in those steps are strength for the farmer to be able to sow and harvest the grain and strength for the one who uses his hands to mix and knead the bread. Jesus is talking about all that. In other words, you are praying for healthy bodies and a healthy environment in which food can grow.

"Give us day by day our daily bread" is a loaded statement. It teaches us to pray, "Thank you, Lord, for keeping

the air in our country pollution-free. Thank you for making us wise people who keep our beaches clean. Thank you for preserving the soil from oil contamination. Thank you for keeping all the nutrients in our soil rich, with no chemicals to harm them." We need to be praying this way. We're not specific enough. We take too much for granted and don't ask God to protect and bless what we need for daily living—not only for our own sake, but also for the sake of others.

FORGIVE US OUR SINS, FOR WE ALSO FORGIVE

"And forgive us our sins, for we also forgive everyone who is indebted to us." Jesus is now dealing with relationships. He says, "Your prayer has to take into consideration those with whom you are in relationship." When you come before God, check to see if anyone has anything against you or if you are holding anything against anyone. Don't come into God's presence and expect to have your prayers answered if you are asking God to forgive you, but you are refusing to forgive others.

Having good relationships is one of the keys to answered prayer.

The gospel of Matthew includes this sobering statement after Jesus' teaching on prayer: *"For if you forgive men when they sin against you, your heavenly Father will also forgive you. But if you do not forgive men their sins, your Father will not forgive your sins"* (Matt. 6:14–15). And if God doesn't forgive you, He's not going to answer your prayer.

We often overlook the importance of our relationships—and how those relationships affect our prayers. The devil uses this tendency against us. We go to church and start singing a few worship songs. Soon we forget that we're angry at others, so we don't determine to make things right. We let the songs cover up our anger. Yet it remains within us. When we go home, we remember what made us angry, and we hold onto that anger until it develops into bitterness. However, as far as Christ is concerned, having good relationships is one of the keys to answered prayer:

Therefore, if you are offering your gift at the altar and there remember that your brother has something against you, leave your gift there in front of the altar. First go and be reconciled to your brother; then come and offer your gift. (Matt. 5:23–24)

We can't do business at a holy altar when we have a bitter heart. We are to forgive freely. *"Peter came to Jesus and asked, 'Lord, how many times shall I forgive my brother when he sins against me? Up to seven times?' Jesus answered, 'I tell you, not seven times, but seventy-seven times'"* (Matt. 18:21–22).

When you pray and fast, God will reveal to you all the hurt, bitterness, and anger you are holding against people. There is going to be conviction in your life because God will remind you of broken relationships you had forgotten about. Why? Because He can talk to you about them now. He can finally get through to you because you're listening.

Perhaps you say, "I have faith to believe that God will answer my prayer," but you're holding on to unforgiveness. The Bible says, *"The only thing that counts is faith expressing itself through love"* (Gal. 5:6). So God will say to you, "Yes, but faith works when love is in order, and you are not living in forgiveness." No matter how much faith you feel you have, if your relationships aren't clear, they will shut down your faith so that it can't work. You need faith to please God (Heb. 11:6), but you also need love, for *"God is love"* (1 John 4:8, 16). Forgiveness will free your prayers so that they can work.

Therefore, find out if your relationships are right. Have you committed a wrong against anybody? Are you holding on to a grudge? Is there anyone in your family or local church, anyone at your job, with whom you aren't in good relationship? God is looking for clean hands and a pure heart (Ps. 24:3–4). A broken and a contrite heart the Lord will not ignore or despise (Ps. 51:17). If we regard iniquity in our hearts, the Lord will not hear us (Ps. 66:18 KJV). However, when we forgive others, God will also forgive us—and the way will be opened for Him to hear and answer our prayers.

DO NOT LEAD US INTO TEMPTATION

Last, Jesus says, *"And do not lead us into temptation, but deliver us from the evil one."* This does not mean that God might steer us toward temptation against our wills. It means that we are to ask God for wisdom so we won't put ourselves into situations that will cause us to compromise our relationship with Him. In other words, we are to ask God for strength and wisdom to stop making bad decisions and to stop going into bad situations that will tempt us to sin. Some of us set ourselves up for trouble; then we ask God to deliver us. God is saying, "When you come before Me, pray for wisdom so you can make good decisions without compromising your life in any way."

When Jesus asked Peter, James, and John to stay with Him while He prayed in the Garden of Gethsemane before His arrest and crucifixion, the disciples fell asleep. *"Could you men not keep watch with me for one hour?"* [Jesus] *asked Peter. "Watch and pray so that you will not fall into temptation. The spirit is willing, but the body is weak"* (Matt. 26:40–41). Jesus knew that Peter was about to be tempted to deny Him—after claiming that he would be willing to die with Him. He told Peter to remain alert and pray. Jesus was referring to watchfulness and prayer when He taught us to pray, *"Do not lead us into temptation."* We need to be alert to the temptations and weaknesses that could harm our relationship with God and our testimony for Him, things that Satan will exploit to cause us to stumble. Then we need to pray that God will protect us from succumbing to them. The Bible says, *"Put on the full armor of God so that you can take your stand against the devil's schemes"* (Eph. 6:11).

YOURS IS THE KINGDOM, POWER, AND GLORY FOREVER

Some of the biblical manuscripts include this benediction at the end of Jesus' teaching on prayer in Matthew's gospel: *"For Yours is the kingdom and the power and the glory forever. Amen"* (Matt. 6:13 NKJV). After you have prayed, then worship the Father again. When you do so, you're saying to God, "I know You're going to answer this prayer; therefore, I'm going to thank You ahead of time. I'm going to give You all the glory that comes from what happens. When the answer is manifested, I'm going to tell everybody that it is because of You." All the power and all the glory belong to God forever.

DID THE DISCIPLES TRULY LEARN JESUS' SECRET?

Jesus' disciples observed His lifestyle of prayer and asked Him to teach them to pray. Do we have any evidence that they learned His secret?

In Acts 1:14, we read that after Jesus was resurrected and had ascended to heaven, the disciples and the other followers of Jesus *"all continued with one accord in prayer and supplication."* They were waiting for the *"power from on high"* (Luke 24:49) that Jesus had promised them—and they were "watching and praying," just as He had taught them. On the Day of Pentecost, God filled the disciples with His Holy Spirit. At the outpouring of the Spirit, three thousand were converted and *"everyone was filled with awe, and many wonders and miraculous signs were done by the apostles"* (Acts 2:42). The disciples' prayers resulted in their receiving the baptism of the Holy Spirit, and their working wonders and signs to God's glory, just as Jesus had done.

Later, we see that the disciples continued to follow the lifestyle of prayer that Jesus had demonstrated for them. They declared, *"We...will give our attention to prayer and the ministry of the word"* (Acts 6:3–4). The entire book of Acts describes how they continued the ministry of Jesus through prayer and the power of the Holy Spirit. They learned the secret to Jesus' effectiveness in ministry. Now that you have learned the same secret, what will you do with it?

LET'S PRAY TOGETHER

Heavenly Father,
Like Jesus' disciples, we, too, need to learn to pray. Thank You for giving us this model prayer so we can know how to pray as Jesus did and be effective in ministry as He was. Your Word says, *"The one who calls you is faithful and he will do it"* (1 Thess. 5:24). You have called us to a lifestyle of prayer, and we ask You to fulfill that calling in us. Give us a heart to seek an intimate relationship with You every day and to follow Your thoughts and ways rather than our own thoughts and ways—or others' opinions. We pray this in the name of Jesus, our Great Intercessor. Amen.

PUTTING PRAYER INTO PRACTICE

Ask yourself:

- Do I seek an intimate relationship with the Father on a daily basis?
- Are my prayers heartfelt expressions of communion with God—or more like a shopping list or rote repetition?
- Am I being effective in my life and ministry so that God's will and kingdom are being done on earth?

Action Steps:

- Over the next few weeks, increase the time you spend with God in prayer each day in order to build a relationship of intimacy with Him.
- Use Jesus' model prayer as a guideline for your prayers. Take each step and personalize it so that it is a heartfelt expression of your growing relationship with God.
- Challenge: Set a goal to spend an hour a day in prayer.

Principles

1. Prayer is more important than all the other activities of the day. Through prayer, God gives guidance, wisdom, and discernment for fulfilling His will and purposes.

2. Through His intimacy with the Father, Jesus knew the thoughts and heart of God and manifested in His ministry what God was doing in the world.

3. God wants the same communion with us that He had with Jesus, so that we will naturally manifest His works.

4. Prayer does not come automatically. It must be learned.

5. Prayer is asking God to accomplish His will in the earth. Christ taught His disciples how to fulfill this purpose by giving them a prayer to use as a pattern or model.

6. The elements of Jesus' model prayer are the following:

   "Our Father": We bring to God the concerns of others as well as ourselves, acknowledging God as our Source.

   "In heaven": We admit we need help from outside our earthly realm—that we need God's help. We depend on Jesus and the Spirit as our intermediaries with God.

   "Hallowed be Your Name": We worship the Father as the Holy One, glorifying all His attributes. We honor Him in our lives and dealings with others.

   "Your kingdom come. Your will be done on earth as it is in heaven": We express interest in God's kingdom and what He wants accomplished before our own interests.

   "Give us day by day our daily bread": We ask God to supply the daily needs of others as well as our own and to provide for the process that makes that sustenance possible.

   "And forgive us our sins, for we also forgive everyone who is indebted to us": We forgive others so that God will also forgive us and will hear and answer our prayers.

   "And do not lead us into temptation, but deliver us from the evil one": We are alert to temptations and weaknesses that Satan will exploit to harm our relationship with God. We pray that God will protect us from succumbing to them.

   "For Yours is the kingdom and the power and the glory forever. Amen": We worship the Father again, giving Him all the glory in advance for answered prayer.

Chapter Seven

Twelve Action Steps to Prayer

Proven principles of prayer from biblical figures whose prayers were powerful and effective.

I n this chapter, I want to show you a useful approach for organizing your steps in prayer. The principles that follow were developed from evaluating the prayer lives of Jesus, Abraham, Joseph, Moses, David, Ezekiel, and others in the Bible. When you study these biblical figures, you see that they all used a similar pattern in prayer. Their prayers received the attention of God and produced powerful results. *"The prayer of a righteous man is powerful and effective"* (James 5:16).

1. BECOME SILENT

First, prayer should begin with silence. We don't normally make a practice of this, but it's a very important aspect of prayer. To be silent means to gather oneself, to be still.

In Matthew 6:6, Jesus said, *"When you pray, go into your room, close the door and pray to your Father, who is unseen. Then your Father, who sees what is done in secret, will reward you."* Jesus is telling us to go to a quiet and private place where we will not be disturbed. In New Testament times, most of the roofs of the houses were flat, and people often prayed on the roof. That was their quiet place. They would go there to get away from all the noise and busyness in the house.

When you begin to enter into prayer, first get quiet and eliminate distractions. You can't pray effectively when all around you the children are playing, the CD player is going, the television is on, and people are asking you questions.

Prayer necessitates collecting yourself—your thoughts, your attention, your concentration. You need silence or isolation, because you have to pull your entire self together. We are usually distracted by many things when we come to prayer. Our bodies are there, but our minds are somewhere else. We might be experiencing all kinds of emotions. Therefore, you need to put yourself in a position where you can become quiet. Let the Lord calm your heart. *"You will keep in perfect peace him whose mind is steadfast, because he trusts in you"* (Isa. 26:3). The word for *"peace"* in Hebrew is *shalom,* which means "more than enough." It means prosperity. Everything you need is provided in God, so you don't have to be distracted by worry when you pray.

Prayer necessitates collecting yourself and coming into a quiet place before God.

This step may take ten minutes, an hour, or five hours, but it is the entrance to prayer. Sometimes you read stories of people praying in the forest for ten hours. How did they do this? You have to read the details of their prayer lives. They spent two or three hours just walking in order to get rid of distracting thoughts. Therefore, when you come before the Lord, in whatever private place you find to do so, get quiet and listen to nothing but God. Let your heart be restful, and come into the quiet place. That's when you are really praying. Too often, we try to rush this process. The Bible says, *"Be still, and know that I am God"* (Ps. 46:10). In this sense, we can say—

> *Prayer is the expression of man's dependency upon God for all things.*

I encourage you to spend time in quiet contemplation before the Lord. It's all right to say nothing. Many times we start talking right away. We're thinking about all the things that happened that day and all kinds of things we've heard. Just become quiet and bring your whole self to prayer. If you are trying to pray, but your spirit, body, mind, and emotions are separated, then you are not one—you are not unified. You will be unable to pray God's will with singleness of purpose. Silence helps bring you into a unity of heart and purpose with yourself and God.

2. GIVE ADORATION

The second step to prayer is adoration. This step corresponds to hallowing God's name, mentioned in Jesus' model prayer. (See Luke 11:2.) Adoration means worshipping God. When you adore someone, you express how precious that person is to you. The first part of Psalm 95 is a good Scripture passage for this purpose. I think it would make a great worship song today. As a matter of fact, you could put your own tune to this psalm and sing it during the day:

> *Come, let us sing for joy to the LORD; let us shout aloud to the Rock of our salvation. Let us come before him with thanksgiving and extol him with music and song. For the LORD is the great God, the great King above all gods. In his hand are the depths of the earth, and the mountain peaks belong to him. The sea is his, for he made it, and his hands formed the dry land. Come, let us bow down in worship, let us kneel before the LORD our Maker; for he is our God and we are the people of his pasture, the flock under his care.*
>
> (Ps. 95:1–7)

What a song of adoration! *"Come, let us bow down in worship."* We are to worship God for who He is: King of all the earth, our Creator, our Savior, our All in All. Start worshipping Him. Start adoring Him. Start blessing Him. Start describing Him. Tell Him how you see Him. You can say, "Lord, You are powerful, great, awesome, omnipotent, matchless. You are God above everyone and everything. You are merciful and wonderful. You are my Counselor. You are perfect. You are abiding. You are never weak. You are eternal. You are above all things and in all things. Everything receives its meaning in You, Lord. You are powerful. There is nothing besides You and no one who can compare with You. You alone are God. You are the only wise God: No one is as wise as You. You are all-knowing: You know everything about me and everyone else. You understand things we don't understand. You are higher and deeper than our problems. We have no problems when You are present. You are all in all, and You are through all; there is no one like You."

3. MAKE CONFESSION

The next step is confession. I taught a course on prayer for Christ for the Nations Ministry every semester for about three years when I was at Oral Roberts University. When I came to this list and taught the students how to go through these steps of prayer, most of them would ask, "Shouldn't we *start* with confession?" I would answer, "If you did so, you wouldn't know what you should confess."

Most of us have been taught that confession means bringing up our past sins, feeling remorse, getting emotional, and so on. That's not the heart of confession. Confession is a very different concept. It means agreeing with God about what He says *to* you and *about* you. You can agree with God only when you can hear what He is saying to you. This brings us back to adoration.

When you enter into God's presence through adoration,

Confession means agreeing with God about what He says *to* you and *about* you.

He is not going to start dealing with other people first. He's going to start shining His light on places you thought He never knew anything about. He's going to bring things into the open. You're going to think, "I hope nobody knows what I'm thinking. If they knew the things God is speaking to me about, they wouldn't stand next to me." God says to us, in effect, "I don't want you to condemn yourself; I want you to tell Me I'm right. Am I right? Is it sin? If it is, then you must agree with Me that it is wrong and stop doing it."

Confession takes place when God points out something in your life and says, "Get rid of that," or "That's rebellion," or "You know you shouldn't have done that," or "That's sin," and you say, "Yes, God, You're right. I won't do that any longer." Then you put your trust in Him to enable you to walk by the Spirit. *"Live by the Spirit, and you will not gratify the desires of the sinful nature"* (Gal. 5:16). When the Holy Spirit shows you something in your life that is not right, then you are to agree with Him. If you disagree with Him, you're not confessing.

Let's look at this step in practical terms. Suppose God points out a particular sin in your life, but you ignore His prompting. Then you go to a prayer meeting, and the Holy Spirit says, "Don't ask Me for anything until you deal with this problem," but you continue praying about other things. The Spirit then says, "You did something wrong, and you haven't dealt with it yet. I want you to fix it tonight." However, you sing and try to drown out the conviction. You're not confessing. When you agree that God is right, that is confessing.

As I wrote earlier, this Scripture was written to believers: *"If we confess our sins, he is faithful and just and will forgive us our sins"* (1 John 1:9). When He forgives us, what else does He do? *"Purify us from all unrighteousness"* (v. 9). The word *righteous* means to be in "right standing" or position with an authority. That means God will cleanse us from everything else that could prevent Him from repositioning us in right standing or alignment with God's perfect will, so that He can bless us.

How does the cleansing come? You have to do something. You have to admit your sin and turn away from it. Telling God you're sorry you did something, while you're planning to do it again, is showing God that you don't agree that it's a problem. *"If we claim we have not sinned, we make him out to be a liar and his word has no place in our lives"* (v. 10).

The Bible says, *"He is faithful and just."* *"Just"* means right. God is saying, "If you agree with what I say is true and that what I have pointed out to you is sin, then I have a right to forgive you because of Jesus' atonement for your sins." In other words, God will respond in a righteous way and forgive you. This means unforgiven sin is sin that you never acknowledge as sin. You keep holding onto it and doing it; therefore, God cannot cleanse you from it.

So adoration leads to spending time in prayer dealing with yourself. Believe me, God has a way of revealing your heart to you if you start this process. The Bible says God dwells in the praises of His people. When you go to a quiet place and get rid of distractions, when you start worshipping God, and He begins to dwell around you, you now have holiness in your presence, and He starts pointing out unholiness. You don't respond by saying, "That isn't really true, Lord." He says, "I can't do business with you if you don't agree with Me. Are you are telling Me that I'm wrong?"

God may even prompt you to call someone, say you're sorry for something you did, and ask for forgiveness. He will say, "Are we going to do business or not? You are holding iniquity in your heart, and I want you to do something about it now." "But, God, You want me to call *him*?" "Look, you don't understand. This thing is blocking your prayer life."

David was one of the worst sinners in the world. He committed adultery, conceived a child out of wedlock, and killed a man. Yet God said, "This is a man after My own heart." (See 1 Samuel 13:14.) Why did God say this about David? If anybody confessed quickly after having his sin pointed out to him, it was David. He was completely honest about his sin. He didn't make excuses; he admitted that he had sinned against God. This amazing thing made his prayer life powerful. Here is his confession, or his agreement with God:

> *Have mercy on me, O God, according to your unfailing love; according to your great compassion blot out my transgressions. Wash away all my iniquity and cleanse me from my sin. For I know my transgressions, and my sin is always before me. Against you, you only, have I sinned and done what is evil in your sight, so that you are proved right when you speak and justified when you judge.* (Ps. 51:1–4)

When David confessed, he said, "*Against you, you only, have I sinned and done what is evil in your sight*" (v. 4). When we sin, we sin against God's nature and character, His purity and righteousness, His love and grace. David confessed, "I have '*done what is evil in your sight, so that you are proved right when you speak and justified when you judge.*' You call it sin, and You are right, God."

If you continue to play with sin and don't agree with God about it, it will destroy you. What you have been desiring in your life will never happen, for you will be the ruination of your own pursuits. Think about what God is saying. Confession doesn't mean merely bringing up your past. It means agreeing with and obeying God immediately when He shows you that you are wrong. Then God will draw near to you. He will say, "I like this person. He's someone after My own heart. He has a mind like Mine. He cannot abide deceit."

If you have done something wrong, confess it quickly. I practice this principle, because it's something I learned early in my life as a believer. I worked as a chaplain at Oral Roberts University for a number of years. My immediate supervisor was the senior chaplain at the school. Over him was the dean of the School of Theology. One day they called me to a meeting, and the three of us were talking **Once God cleanses you, there isn't anyone who can condemn you.** about something that had gone wrong in my department. I had done something that was not right in order to try to help someone. I sat there trying to explain why I had done it. In the midst of my explanation, the dean stopped me and said, "Hold it. Don't ever do that if you want God to bless you." I said, "Do what?" He said, "Whatever you justify, you have not repented of. Whatever you explain, you are not sorry for. Just say, 'I was wrong; forgive me,' and ask God to forgive you. This meeting should have been over in two minutes. You're making this a long meeting and also messing up your life. Don't carry this habit out of this office."

If you ever find that you are wrong, just confess it, agree, ask for forgiveness, and go on with your life. Whatever you justify, you cannot repent of. Maybe you're justifying why you fell back into a certain sin. Instead, just say, "God, forgive me. I was wrong. I'm back home." Don't go into a long, drawn-out explanation about why you sinned and all the ramifications. God asks you, "Is it sin?" "Yes." "Good. You agree with Me that it's sin; now, I will forgive you. I will cleanse you from all unrighteousness. Let Me clean you up." God is faithful. Once God cleanses you, there isn't anyone who can condemn you. *"Who will bring any charge against those whom God has chosen? It is God who justifies. Who is he that condemns?"* (Rom. 8:33–34).

4. GIVE THANKS

After you've confessed, start giving thanks. *"Be joyful always; pray continually; give thanks in all circumstances, for this is God's will for you in Christ Jesus"* (1 Thess. 5:16–18). Thanksgiving is God's will for us.

Of course, now that you have confessed, you can give thanks abundantly because your heart is free. God not only gives you freedom, but He also gives you something to be thankful for. He just forgave you of your sin. You have enough to be thankful for to last hours.

David was thinking of thanksgiving even as he confessed. *"Save me from bloodguilt, O God, the God who saves me, and my tongue will sing of your righteousness. O Lord, open my lips, and my mouth will declare your praise"* (Ps. 51:14–15). That's the way to pray. As a matter of fact, this confession psalm ends in worship. *"The sacrifices of God are a broken spirit; a broken and contrite heart, O God, you will not despise....Then there will be righteous sacrifices, whole burnt offerings to delight you; then bulls will be offered on your altar"* (vv. 17, 19). Offering sacrifices and burnt offerings was an Old Testament method of worship. If you have confessed before God, then your heart is right, and you can offer sacrifices of praise to God. (See Hebrews 13:15.)

5. MAKE SUPPLICATION

The next step is to make supplication. Philippians 4:6 says, *"Do not be anxious about anything, but in everything, by prayer and petition [*"supplication"* NKJV], with thanksgiving, present your requests to God."*

"Supplication" is a word that implies three things. It means to intercede, to petition, and to brood. By brooding, I mean a deep passion. When you offer supplication, it means you feel the heart of God. You desire His will so much until it becomes an emotional experience. This is

usually when you begin to weep in prayer or pray more fervently. It's an emotionally overwhelming experience of God. God shows you some of what He's feeling, and you become unified with His purposes and desires. Supplication is a natural outgrowth of thanksgiving. When you give thanks, you usually move into supplication because thanksgiving pleases God, and He reveals to you what is in His heart.

6. SPECIFY PETITIONS AND REQUESTS

The next step is to specify your petitions. Prayer is not just mumbo jumbo. It is a very articulate, intentional communication. It is an art. A lawyer does much studying before he stands before a judge and jury to present his case. That's what you pay him to do. He does his research so he can bring information pertinent to the case. A common thing you hear a prosecutor or defense

Prayer needs to be intentional and practical.

lawyer say is, "Irrelevant!" When you come before God to petition for things that you want Him to do, you have to be sure the evidence you bring is relevant to the case. This is why God has so many names. You need to address Him specifically for your particular petitions.

If you want peace, you appeal to Him as Jehovah-Shalom (The Lord our Peace), rather than Jehovah-Jireh (The Lord our Provider). If you need healing, He is Jehovah-Rapha (The Lord our Healer). "Lord, I need You to be Jehovah-Rapha specifically in this case. I am appealing to the court for healing. I don't need a car right now; I can't even drive it. I need to be healed. You say that if I love You and follow Your commands, *'the LORD will take away from* [me] *all sickness'* (Deut. 7:15 NKJV)."

Therefore, specify your petitions by acknowledging God's name and Word. One way to do this is to write down the things you want to pray for; next to those items, write down the Scriptures that you're going to use when you pray. Again, prayer needs to be intentional and practical. It's not something you throw together. It's good to have things written down specifically. Then, when you pray about your list of petitions, God will know that there is thought and intention behind your requests. When you pray for each request, you are praying according to God's Word, and God will send help for each request. *"This is the confidence we have in approaching God: that if we ask anything **according to his will**, he hears us. And if we know that he hears us—whatever we ask—we know that we have what we asked of him"* (1 John 5:14–15, emphasis added).

7. SECURE THE PROMISES

The next step is related to the previous one: Secure your promises. *"For no matter how many promises God has made, they are 'Yes' in Christ. And so through him the 'Amen' is spoken by us to the glory of God"* (2 Cor. 1:20). Hold onto God's promises as you take His Word before Him, applying it to the particular request you are making.

When Jesus wanted to minister to people, He never assumed what they needed. He asked them, *"What do you want me to do for you?"* (Matt. 20:32). God answers specific requests based on His promises. Let's look at an example of this.

Bartimaeus was blind, and he was begging by the side of the road. When he heard that Jesus was coming, he said, *"Jesus, Son of David, have mercy on me!"* (Mark 10:47). Jesus came to him and said, *"What do you want me to do for you?"* (v. 51). You might think that would have been obvious. Yet there are some people who would rather remain in the condition they're in. Jesus had people tell Him what they specifically wanted. *"The blind man said, 'Rabbi, I want to see.' 'Go,' said Jesus, 'your faith has healed you.' Immediately he received his sight and followed Jesus along the road."*

Bartimaeus was healed because he asked for healing based on his legal rights. He was crying out, *"Son of David"* (Mark 10:47–48). That's a legal statement. Abraham's covenant came through David. Scripture says the Messiah will come through David's line and that David's throne will last forever (Isa. 9:6–7). Bartimaeus reasoned, "If Jesus is the Messiah, He must be the Son of David. If He is the Son of David, then every covenant promise God made to Abraham, Moses, and David can come to me through Him." So he said, *'Son of David, have mercy on me!'* (Mark 10:47–48). *"'Go,' said Jesus, 'your faith has healed you'"* (v. 52). The man deserved healing because he petitioned specifically through the promises. Likewise, we are to secure the promises when we pray.

Now let's look at a case in the Bible in which a person who was healed didn't ask Jesus for healing but was still healed based on the promises. One day, on the Sabbath, Jesus walked into a synagogue. There was a woman sitting in the crowd who had a problem with her back. Jesus stood up and read the Scriptures. When He finished, He looked at the crowd and saw the woman. The Bible says she was hunched over. She couldn't even lift herself up. Jesus then set His eyes on her, called her to Him, put His hands on her, and healed her. The Bible says, *"Immediately she straightened up and praised God"* (Luke 13:13).

The leader of the temple and other religious leaders began to murmur among themselves, saying, "How dare He heal her on the Sabbath day!" Jesus turned to them and said, *"Should not this woman, a daughter of Abraham, whom Satan has kept bound for eighteen long years, be set free on the Sabbath day from what bound her?"* (Luke 13:16).

What was Jesus doing? He was pulling out files of evidence. Somehow, we have the impression that if we look sick, God will feel sorry for us and heal us. Yet even though this woman looked terrible, she wasn't healed until the legal action was in place. Jesus said, *"Should not this woman, a **daughter of Abraham**...."* That was a powerful statement. In other words, she had a right to be delivered and healed, according to God's promise.

God heals us because we give Him evidence that it is our legal right based on His promises.

Jesus didn't heal her just because it was the Sabbath. He healed her because, in the contract God had made with His chosen people on behalf of Abraham, He had said, *"The LORD will take away from you all sickness"* (Deut. 7:15).

We ask the Lord to heal us because we're hurting, and He does have compassion on us to heal us. (See Matthew

14:14.) However, the primary reason He heals us is that we give Him evidence that it is our legal right.

8. PLEAD THE CASE

Next, plead your case. Let's look more closely at what it means to "plead." Pleading your case does not mean begging and moaning and becoming emotional. God isn't impressed with any of that. When you yell and scream, all you get is tired. You don't get answers. Again, prayer is a legal art. It is something you do because you rightfully deserve what you are asking for based on God's promises.

In Luke 18, Jesus said to His disciples, in effect, "Let Me teach you not only how to pray, but also how to get answers." (See verse 1.) He revealed how to go all the way in prayer until we see God.

Jesus began by saying, *"In a certain town there was a judge who neither feared God nor cared about men"* (v. 2). This is God teaching on prayer, and He tells us, "To illustrate, think about someone who doesn't even care about God and has no regard for your situation. Imagine having to ask this type of person for something." He used the worst example of a source. I think He wanted to illustrate the fact that prayer doesn't have anything to do with God liking you or not liking you. We say, "Lord, if You love me, bless me." God answers, "I bless you because of two things: first, you qualify through faith in My promises and righteous living; and second, I am holy; therefore, I keep My Word."

Jesus then continued, *"And there was a widow in that town who kept coming to him with the plea, 'Grant me justice against my adversary'"* (v. 3). The reason He used the example of a widow is that, in Jesus' day, a widow was someone who had really hit rock-bottom in life. In the Israelite culture, if a married man died, his brother had to marry the man's widow, care for her, and protect his brother's name so she didn't have to go on the street and beg and bring disgrace to the family name. If the second brother died, the third one had to marry her, and so on. Thus, when a woman became a widow, it was because there weren't any more brothers. There were no more relatives to care for her and help her.

Therefore, when God taught us about prayer, He used the worst case scenario to describe not only the one who is to answer the prayer, but also the one who is praying. Let me tell you why the widow is important to this illustration. God wants you to come to prayer with an attitude that says, "You're the only One who can help me." Often, we pray for God's help, but we have a backup plan, just in case. God says, "You can pray all you want. I'm not going to answer until you have no other place to turn. Then you will know that I am your Provider."

God wants you to come to prayer with an attitude that says, "You're the only One who can help me."

God doesn't want to be used as a spare tire. We say, "If I can't get help from anyone else, I'll ask God." God says, "Wait a minute. I am not an option." This woman had no option, no alternative. Sometimes we find ourselves in similar situations: "Lord, if You don't help me, I'm going to lose this house." We need to depend completely on Him.

Jesus went on to say, *"For some time* [the judge] *refused"* (v. 4). How long? It doesn't say. When we pray, sometimes the answer doesn't come right away, but that doesn't mean it's not on the way. People may ask you, "How long are you going to believe it's going to happen?" "For some time." "How long?" "For some time." "How long is that?" "I don't know. I'm going to hold on until I see it, because the pure in heart will see God. Without holiness, without single-mindedness, no one will see the salvation of God."

Jesus concluded His story with, *"Finally* [the judge] *said to himself, 'Even though I don't fear God or care about men, yet because this widow keeps bothering me, I will see that she gets justice, so that she won't eventually wear me out with her coming!'"* (vv. 4–5). Did the judge say, "I will see that she gets a break"? No, he used a legal word. *"I will see that she gets justice* [what is rightfully hers].*"*

God cannot lie. Therefore, what He has promised has to come to pass. It is the integrity of His name and His Word that calls us to be persistent in prayer. *"God is not a man, that he should lie, nor a son of man, that he should change his mind. Does he speak and then not act? Does he promise and not fulfill?"* (Num. 23:19).

Jesus then explained the parable: *"Listen to what the unjust judge says. And will not God bring about justice for his **chosen ones**, who cry out to him day and night? Will he keep putting them off? I tell you, he will see that they get justice, and quickly"* (vv. 6–8, emphasis added). Jesus was saying, "If a man who doesn't acknowledge God or His righteousness has to see to it that a woman he doesn't like gets what she deserves, how much more will God, who loves you, see to it that you get justice—and quickly." In other words, God isn't going to take as long as that judge who didn't like people. He will give justice to His chosen ones, those who have received His promises as a spiritual inheritance.

Jesus added, *"However, when the Son of Man comes, will he find faith on the earth?"* (v. 8). Faith is believing the promises. People pray, but they don't want to believe until *after* the answer comes. This parable tells us that when we believe God's Word and repeat His promises back to Him, God says, "I'm going to answer you—not because I 'like' you, but because I am holy." Therefore, plead your case based on God's Word and integrity.

9. BELIEVE

This is a difficult one for many of us: Believe. As in the parable of the unjust judge we just looked at, God says that after we plead, we are to believe. Asking, in itself, doesn't cause you to receive.

Read carefully the words of Christ in this passage from Mark 11. This is another mini-seminar on prayer:

"Have faith in God," Jesus answered. "I tell you the truth, if anyone says to this mountain, 'Go, throw yourself into the sea,' and does not doubt in his heart but believes that what he says will happen, it will be done for him. Therefore I tell you, whatever you ask for in prayer, believe...." (vv. 22–24)

142

What's the next phrase? *"...that you have received it."* Do you see the *"-ed"* on *"received"*? When you ask, believe right then and there that you have already received it. It is possible to ask for something in prayer and not believe. We do it all the time. We usually give up too soon.

In the book of Daniel, we read that Daniel prayed and that, the same day he prayed, the answer was on its way. However, Daniel didn't know that. (See Daniel 10:10–14; 9:23). What did Daniel do? He kept praying. After twenty-one days, an angel arrived with the answer. The point is, Daniel didn't say, "Well, it's been ten days now. This thing doesn't work. I'm going back to doing what I had been do-ing." No. Daniel believed that if God said something, it was supposed to happen. He wasn't going to stop praying until it was manifested. He was going to persevere until he saw it with his own eyes.

Do you believe that what you prayed last night is going to happen? I want you to confess something. Say, "Lord, I believe." You might not be a believer all the way. Maybe you tend to doubt. When you start doubting, though, be honest, like the father of the demon-possessed boy, and say, *"Lord, I believe; help my unbelief!"* (Mark 9:24 NKJV). That's a good prayer. We can't let doubt enter into our prayers. It will short-circuit them.

> *If any of you lacks wisdom, he should ask God, who gives generously to all without finding fault, and it will be given to him. But when he asks, he must be-lieve and not doubt, because he who doubts is like a wave of the sea, blown and tossed by the wind. That man should not think he will receive anything from the Lord.* (James 1:5–7)

Instead, when you believe that you *have received* what you asked for, it will be yours.

10. GIVE THANKS

After you have believed, offer thanksgiving again. Let's compare the two thanksgivings. There is a progression in prayer. The first thanksgiving expresses your appreciation for God's forgiveness and mercy. The second thanksgiving is the highest form of faith. You thank God for what you don't yet see because you believe it is already done. That takes faith. If you truly believe that when you prayed, you received what you asked for, then you will start thanking Him. We are not to wait until we see the manifestation of our answers before expressing our gratitude.

In fact, you don't show God that you really believe until you thank Him. We do this for humans, but we don't do it for God. For instance, suppose you go to the bank and talk to the manager about getting a loan. The banker approves the loan and says, "Consider it done. The money will be deposited to your account." You don't see the money. You don't know if he did it or not. Yet what do you say? "Thank you very much." Then you go and do your business based on the banker's word. God says, "Do the same for Me. Thank Me before it is even registered on your account statement." Why? If we will believe God, then the answer will come.

Close all your prayer times with thanksgiving because what you have asked for has already been received.

Oftentimes, we block the answers to our prayers. The answer was coming, but we walked away, saying, "I'm not wasting my time believing that anymore." What happens then? *"That man should not think he will receive anything from the Lord"* (James 1:7).

Don't block your prayers. Start giving thanks, and thank God until the answer manifests itself. If someone asks you tomorrow, "How are you doing?" just say, "I'm thanking Him for what I have received." If you are asked, "How are you feeling?" say, "I'm feeling really good." "Why?" "I'm thanking God for what is going to be manifested." When you respond like that, you start attracting angels. The Bible says, *"Are not all angels ministering spirits sent to serve those who will inherit salvation?"* (Heb. 1:14).

You can close all your prayer times with thanksgiving because what you have asked for has already been received. It just hasn't been revealed yet for other people to see.

11. LIVE IN EXPECTATION

Continue in a spirit of thanksgiving by living in expectation of the answer to your prayer. Don't forget what you have prayed. My life has changed as I have personally applied this principle. More and more as I walk with the Lord, He teaches me foundational truths that make a significant difference in my life. If you believe you are going to be blessed financially, if you expect God to bless you, then I suggest you do something similar to what I did. Several years ago, I said to my banker, "I want to open a new account." He said, "For what?" I said, "For something I expect." I have several different accounts in that bank, but I said, "This one is different. This is my blessing account. I'm expecting God to bless me, and I'm going to prove to Him that I expect it by actually giving Him somewhere to put it. If I put it in my checking account, I might not keep it. If I put it in the loan account, it might get lost. I'm going to give God a target where He can aim the blessings." After I opened that account, I had more money in my life than ever before.

Many times, people come to me and say, "Pastor Myles, I'm praying for a job." I say, "How many applications have you filled out?" "Well, I'm waiting for the Lord to lead me to something." Of course, we need to follow God's leading, but too often we're lazy and don't believe. We need to knock. If you believe that God will give you a job, then fill out every application you can, because God is going to bring one of them to you. If the employer doesn't know you're there, how can he call you for an interview?

Live in expectation. If you ask God to provide you with a car so you can drive to church to worship Him and you believe God heard you, then go shopping. Don't go back to church saying, "Well, the Lord will arrange it." Go to the car lot and look around. Why? You expect God to do something. Perhaps you are praying for a spouse. Look your best. That person might show up today. If you don't expect, that means you don't believe. Make arrangements for your answer. Perhaps you are praying for new furniture. Believe God, then make room for it in your house. Do you need God to bless you with some new clothes this year? Start giving your old clothes away. If somebody asks, "What are you doing?" say, "I'm making room for my answer." Ephesians 3:20 says, *"Now to him who is able to do immeasurably more than all we ask or imagine, according to his power that is at work within us."*

12. Practice Active Belief

The last step is to practice active belief, which shows you are living in expectation. It is what Jesus meant by "seeking and knocking." In Luke 11:1, when the disciples asked, *"Lord, teach us to pray,"* Jesus proceeded to teach them a model prayer. The ninth verse is part of His discourse on prayer: *"So I say to you: Ask and it will be given to you; seek and you will find; knock and the door will be opened to you."*

Jesus is telling us, "Don't stop after you pray. Get up and go look for what you asked for. You will find it if you seek it. It may be behind some closed doors. If that is the case, then knock." If you believe it is yours, or it is supposed to be yours, or it is rightfully yours, no door or barrier can stop what God has for you. When the devil tries to hold it back, just keep persisting until the door falls down. According to the Word of God, if you knock, it will come to pass. This is the meaning of active prayer.

No door or barrier can stop what God has for you.

Again, if you are believing God for a new house, then go looking. Drive around the neighborhoods that have the kind of house you want. Use your faith in proportion to your confession. Say, "God, I believe You for this." Then go seeking. Call realtors and ask, "What do you have on the market?" Ask people who live in the area that you like to let you know about any of their neighbors who might be putting their houses on the market.

Sometimes the answer might come in the form of goods that have been repossessed from their former owners. Let me explain what the Lord shared with me about repossessed things. When the Israelites came into the Promised Land, they needed a home. The Canaanites were already living there. Why did God drive them out and move Israel in? It is because the Canaanites were the most diabolical, pagan, evil people in the Bible. Thousands of babies died every year by the hands of the Canaanite priests. When a Canaanite wanted good luck, he would take his baby to the priest to be sacrificed. The blood of the child would fall to the ground, and so the land had been corrupted by the Canaanites' practices. They lost the land because they abused it. This basic principle holds true today. There are people who haven't been living right, and so their property has been taken away. God is going to give their property to the righteous.

However, take note: This property needs to be used to bless not only ourselves, but also others, because we, too, could get moved out. Remember what happened when the Israelites began to corrupt the land with their abominations? God said, in effect, "I'm going to scatter you out of the land." Yet He also said, "If you obey Me, I'll bring you back." (See Nehemiah 1:8–9.)

Therefore, practice active belief and continue to live before God in holiness and truth. God will bless you as you ask, seek, and knock.

GROW IN GRACE AND KNOWLEDGE

As you learn how to pray according to biblical principles, you will become a powerfully effective believer. Use these twelve action steps as a guide to prayer, and make sure everything in your life is in order according to God's will and purposes. I'm excited about what God is going to do in your life as you apply these principles and as you grow in the grace and knowledge of God and His ways.

LET'S PRAY TOGETHER

Heavenly Father,
Thank you for giving us principles for prayer in Your Word. Psalm 119:15 says, *"I meditate on your precepts and consider your ways."* Don't allow us to walk away from Your truths and forget them. Help us to study these principles and consider carefully Your ways as revealed in Your Word. Then encourage us to step out in faith to put these principles into practice in our lives. As we do, we thank you for answering our prayers and doing *"immeasurably more than all we ask or imagine, according to* [Your] *power that is at work within us"* (Eph. 3:20). We pray this in the name of Jesus, the Mediator of the new covenant. Amen.

PUTTING PRAYER INTO PRACTICE

Ask yourself:

- Do I take the time to quiet myself before the Lord prior to prayer, or do I usually pray hurriedly, just to get through one more task in my day?
- Do I pray sporadically and haphazardly, or do I pray purposefully according to God's Word?
- Is there any sin in my life that I am trying to justify?

Action Steps:

- This week, gradually begin incorporating the twelve action steps into your prayers.
- If you have been justifying wrongdoing in your life, agree with God that it is sin and truly repent by turning from it and asking God to cleanse you from all unrighteousness. (See 1 John 1:9.)
- Take one thing you are praying for, start living in expectation of it, and practice active belief. Anticipate that what you pray for according to God's Word will happen, and make arrangements for the answer.

Principles

The twelve action steps to prayer are—

1. *Become Silent:* Be still, and gather yourself. If your spirit, body, mind, and emotions are separated, then you will be unable to pray God's will with singleness of purpose. Silence helps bring you into unity with God.

2. *Give Adoration:* Worship God for who He is: King of all the earth, your Creator, your Savior, your All in All.

3. *Make Confession:* Agree with God about what He says to you and about you. Don't dwell on past sins but obey God immediately when He shows you that you are wrong.

4. *Give Thanks:* Offer sacrifices of praise to God with a free heart for all that He has done for you.

5. *Make Supplication:* As God shows you what He desires, wholeheartedly agree with Him in prayer to fulfill His will.

6. *Specify Petitions and Requests:* When you ask God to do something for you, bring evidence relevant to the case—in the form of God's will and Word—through specific, intentional communication.

7. *Secure the Promises:* When you petition the Lord, take God's promises before Him, applying them to the specific request you are making. Then hold onto God's promises.

8. *Plead the Case:* Don't beg or moan before God, but pray intelligently because you rightfully deserve the answer based on God's promises.

9. *Believe:* Believe right at the time you are asking that you have the answer to your request, and you will receive it.

10. *Give Thanks:* Thank God for what you don't yet see because you believe it is already done.

11. *Live in Expectation:* Anticipate the answers to your prayers by preparing the way for them.

12. *Practice Active Belief:* Don't stop after you have prayed. Get up and look for what you asked for. If you seek and knock, it will come to pass.

Chapter Eight

Hurdles to Answered Prayer

Recognizing and overcoming hurdles to answered prayer will protect your prayer potential and give you the right motivation and perspective for prayer.

P rayer is the greatest opportunity and privilege offered to a person in Christ. Yet because of the power of prayer, the adversary makes it his business to see that the prayers of individuals and churches are ineffective. Satan knows that a church is only as powerful as its prayer life. Therefore, he will use misconceptions about prayer to thwart our prayer potential. These misconceptions are hurdles to overcome as we address the problems that lead to unanswered prayer.

Some of these hurdles may be familiar friends to you if you have accepted them and lived with them for any length of time. This can make them hard to recognize—and even harder to set aside. I want to clearly delineate a number of mistaken beliefs about prayer in this chapter so you can see how they differ from the definition of prayer that is based on the Word of God. Rising above these hurdles through God's grace will enable you to truly understand the purpose and power of prayer.

1. LEARNING ABOUT PRAYER, BUT NOT PRACTICING IT

The first hurdle is a desire to just read about the Bible and prayer rather than to study the Word itself and equip oneself for prayer. We gain a false sense of satisfaction when we learn *about* something, but don't actually *do* it. We think it's a part of our lives, but it hasn't made it from our heads to our hearts, from theory to practice. Satan loves it when we read about what we should be doing, but never do it; when we buy books on prayer and the Bible, but never follow what the books say; when we buy teaching tapes, but never practice what the tapes teach. It is like buying a cookbook but never cooking anything from it. How many cookbooks do people have in their homes that they have never used? Many Christians read in the Bible about how believers received answers to their prayers, and they feel inspired. They may say, "Daniel prayed, Joseph prayed, and look at the results they had. *'The prayer of a righteous man is powerful and effective'* (James 5:16). I should pray, too." However, they never make the commitment to do it.

We often have the false idea that if we *know* a great deal about prayer, somehow we *have* prayed. For example, you may have grasped important truths about prayer for the first time through reading this book. You may be saying, "This is powerful. This can change my life." However, if you don't apply these principles to your life, your knowledge won't help you spiritually. *A major cause of unanswered prayer is our becoming experts in the knowledge of prayer but not masters in the practice of praying.* The best approach to prayer is *to pray.*

2. MENTAL ASSENT RATHER THAN ACTION

This hurdle is a variation of the previous one. Mental assent looks so much like faith that many people cannot see the difference between the two. Mental assent means intellectually accepting the Word as true—admiring it and agreeing with it—but not allowing it to have an impact on you, so that it doesn't do you any good. In essence, mental assent *agrees* with God but does not *believe* God.

Mental assent *agrees* with God but does not *believe* God.

The mental assentor affirms that the entire Bible came from God, that it is God's revelation, and that every word of it is true. When a crisis comes, however, he says, "Yes, I believe the Bible is true, but it doesn't work for *me*." He often quotes Scriptures he doesn't really believe. For example, he might mentally affirm the promise, *"God will supply all my needs according to His riches in glory by Christ Jesus"*

(Phil. 4:19 NKJV), but never trust God to do so by making personal application of this verse to his own life.

A person who mentally assents to God's Word says, "Lord, what You said is wonderful!"—and leaves it at that. I can imagine God replying, "Thank you. Now will you please do it?" Such a person may be successful in knowing much about the Word, but as far as His spiritual life is concerned, he has failed. The true believer is a doer of the Word and not a hearer only (James 1:23). The believer builds on rock, while the mental assentor builds on sand. (See Matthew 7:24–27.)

The only way God's promises will become a reality in your life is for you to act on them—and you can't act on them without faith. As a matter of fact, the very word *promise* requires faith. If I promise you something, that means you don't have it yet, so you have to believe I will give it to you. Everything God said He will give us are the "promises of God." God says to us, "I promise I will do this for you, but in reality, it's already done. I want you to believe that what I promise is real. It is already accomplished, because I back up every promise I make."

A variation of mental assent is "sense knowledge." This is the attitude that says, "If I cannot see it, then it is not real. I'll believe it when I see it." The Bible tells us, *"We walk by faith, not by sight"* (2 Cor. 5:7 KJV). This means that faith and sense knowledge are not compatible. Faith is the substance and evidence of things that your sense knowledge cannot see. (See Hebrews 11:1.) Sense knowledge has become one of our biggest obstacles to faith because, in many cultures, we are trained and conditioned to live by our five senses alone. If we cannot analyze something and empirically conclude that it actually works, then we do not believe it is real. However, God says what He has promised is already a reality. Yet it won't become a manifested reality in our lives until we believe it is real *before* we see it—through fully trusting Him and His Word. That's how faith operates.

Again, the Bible says, *"Faith is the substance of things hoped for, the evidence of things not seen"* (Heb. 11:1 KJV). Note carefully that this verse does *not* say that faith is the evidence of things that do not exist. It says that faith is the evidence of *things you cannot see.* For example, you cannot always see how God will meet your need. However, God says, "It's already met; believe Me." That is living by faith. If you live by any other means, you will have high blood pressure, depression, and fear. You will live in frustration because you will to try to figure out how to meet your own needs when you don't have that capability. God says, "I will supply all your needs. I have everything worked out. Trust Me to do it."

If you have been mentally assenting to the truth but not acting on it, you have been living below your privilege for too long. You need to start living by the faith that God gave you so that His Word can come to pass in your life. People say, "Well, I need more faith." Faith is easy to obtain. Faith comes by hearing the Word of God (Rom. 10:17). When you receive the Word, your faith grows. Every time you read the Word or hear good teaching and put it into practice, your spiritual life is strengthened a little more. You don't receive the Word of God without being changed for the better. The Word is the seed. Once you put the seed in good soil, the seed is going to grow because the power is in the seed.

> **If you have been only mentally assenting to the truth, you have been living below your privilege.**

James 1:22 says, *"Do not merely listen to the word, and so deceive yourselves. Do what it says."* This verse separates mental assent from faith. James said if you think listening to the Word by itself will make a difference, you are deceiving yourself. You must learn to apply what you have heard by believing and then acting upon it.

Jesus said to the chief priests and elders of the people,

> *"What do you think? There was a man who had two sons. He went to the first and said, 'Son, go and work today in the vineyard.' 'I will not,' he answered, but later he changed his mind and went. Then the father went to the other son and said the same thing. He answered, 'I will, sir,' but he did not go. Which of the two did what his father wanted?" "The first," they answered.* (Matt. 21:28–31)

The second son mentally assented to do what his father asked, but he never took any action on it. Although the first son was initially rebellious, he ended up agreeing to his father's request and doing it. Jesus was showing us that we cannot just say we believe. We have to live out our faith by doing what God asks. We should not only agree with His Word and will, but also live it.

3. HEARING THE WORD, BUT NOT ABSORBING IT

Another major hurdle to answered prayer is hearing the Word but not absorbing it into one's life. Skipping that step is detrimental to our spiritual health because we must internalize the Word if it is going to make an impact on our lives. When we don't absorb the Word, it often goes in one ear and out the other. Satan steals it away so that it can't have an impact on our relationship with God. Jesus said, *"When anyone hears the message about the kingdom and does not understand it, the evil one comes and snatches away what was sown in his heart"* (Matt. 13:19).

The above statement is part of the parable of the sower. In this parable, the Word of God is depicted as seed, while various types of human attitudes are represented by different types of soil. When the seed is sown along the path— that is, when the Word does not become a central part of a person's life—the enemy comes immediately to steal it. In his attempt to destroy the work of God in our lives, the enemy isn't at first concerned about our money or health. Those things are not as important as the source of our spiritual life—the Word.

Christ said the enemy comes *immediately* to steal the Word of God. This means that even as you are reading this book, the enemy is trying to steal God's truth from you. I imagine he is saying, "If they ever really apply this book, I'm in trouble." That is why the critical juncture for you, in terms of benefit to your spiritual life, is not so much while you are reading this book as it is when you are about to return to other activities. If you don't consciously apply these truths to your life, the enemy will try to make you forget what you've just read. When you start preparing a meal, watching the news on television, or conversing with other people, they will suddenly be gone unless you internalize them.

Jesus often ended His teachings by saying, *"He who has ears to hear, let him hear!"* (See, for example, Matthew 13:9 NKJV; Mark 7:16 NKJV; Luke 14:35 NKJV.) There is physical hearing, and there is spiritual hearing. Jesus knew that the people were listening to His words. However, He told them, in essence, "My words need to become established in your hearts." If we do this, we will be blessed:

> *Anyone who listens to the word but does not do what it says is like a man who looks at his face in a mirror and, after looking at himself, goes away and immediately forgets what he looks like. But the man who looks intently into the perfect law that gives freedom, and continues to do this, not forgetting what he has heard, but doing it—he will be blessed in what he does.*
>
> (James 1:23–25)

I like how *The Living Bible* paraphrases Jesus' command in Revelation 2:7: *"Let this message sink into the ears of anyone who listens to what the Spirit is saying to the churches."* Let the message sink in. Stay focused after you've heard or read the Word, and let it truly sink into your spirit. The Bible calls this process *meditation*. Meditation was an important and valued spiritual exercise in both the Old and New Testaments. Most believers don't practice meditation so they lose much benefit from what they read in the Bible. Perhaps this is due to a misunderstanding of the word *meditation*. Biblical meditation in very different from transcendental meditation, a practice of eastern religions. Transcendental meditation involves chanting and incantation, while biblical meditation focuses solely on God's Word.

Meditation means letting the Word truly sink into your spirit.

When it came time for Joshua to become the leader of the Israelites, the Lord said to him, *"Do not let this Book of the Law depart from your mouth; meditate on it day and night, so that you may be careful to do everything written in* it." He added, *"Then you will be prosperous and successful"* (Josh. 1:8). How would Joshua become prosperous and successful? By meditating on the Word so that it became a part of his life and practice.

After the apostle Paul instructed Timothy in God's ways, he said, *"Meditate on these things; give yourself entirely to them, that your progress may be evident to all"* (1 Tim. 4:15). The Greek word for *"meditate"* in this verse is *meletao,* which means to "revolve in the mind." Biblical mediation is not a mindless process of chanting but of *using* your mind—turning something over and over in your mind in order to understand all its truths and implications—and then embracing those truths by applying them to your whole life.

Meditation may also be compared to the process of rumination, such as when a cow chews its cud. A cow has two stomachs. The first stomach takes in the food that the cow eats and holds it. When the cow is full, it finds a nice, cool place on the grass where it sits down and ruminates. It brings the food back up into its mouth and chews it again. Rumination is the process by which the cow's food is digested; it puts it into a form that can be assimilated into the cow's system through a second stomach. In this way, the food can become strength and life to the animal.

The Bible says we also must undergo a twofold process in order to absorb the Word of God into our lives. The first process is receiving the Word. When you read the Bible or hear a biblical teaching, the Word is initially sown in your "first stomach"—your heart. (See Matthew 13:19.) To receive spiritual strength and life from it, however, you must meditate on it, "digesting" it so that it can permeate your entire being. One advantage we have today, which can help with such "digesting," is the availability of recorded materials that we can listen to multiple times to receive the full benefit from them.

Note carefully: Satan never wants you to get to the meditation stage because that is when the Word of God can become the means for answered prayer. Just sitting down and listening to a good teaching on Sunday morning or Wednesday night is not your key to success. Absorbing the

Word is. Remember that *"when anyone hears the message about the kingdom and does not understand it, the evil one comes and snatches away what was sown in his heart"* (Matt. 13:19). God says, *"I am watching to see that my word is fulfilled"* (Jer. 1:12). If Satan can steal the Word from you, he can steal what God has given you to fulfill His purposes in your life.

Sometimes, right after church, well-meaning people will come and talk to you about things that aren't related to the pastor's message, and it will change your whole focus and attitude. I often ask my congregation to spend a few moments at the end of the service in prayer and meditation so we can think about what the Lord has just taught us and so it can become a part of our lives. When that happens, the devil can't stop the Word, because God now has something He can use to accomplish His will.

4. HOPING RATHER THAN HAVING FAITH

Another hurdle that blocks many people's prayers is "hoping" rather than having faith. There are two ways in which the idea of hope can interfere with what God wants to accomplish through prayer: (1) when we apply the biblical definition of hope (future fulfillment) to present-day faith situations; and (2) when our hope is not the biblical kind but is really just wishful thinking.

First, many people mistake hope for faith. However, they are distinct concepts. The Bible says, *"And now these three remain: faith, hope and love. But the greatest of these is love"* (1 Cor. 13:13). Remember the Greek word for *"faith"* is *pistis,* meaning "belief" or "confidence." It can also mean "conviction" or "assurance." The word for *"hope"* is *elpis,* meaning "expectation" or "confidence." Biblical hope is based on faith because it is the confident anticipation of the ultimate fulfillment of that faith.

Hope is a beautiful and necessary thing when it is about heaven, the second coming of Christ, and everything God has promised us in the future—the culmination of our salvation, the resurrection of our bodies, the new heaven and earth, and our reigning with Jesus forever. The assurance of future blessings is what biblical hope is all about: *"We have this hope as an anchor for the soul, firm and secure"* (Heb. 6:19). *"May the God of hope fill you with all joy and peace as you trust in him, so that you may overflow with hope by the power of the Holy Spirit"* (Rom. 15:13). However, this kind of hope can become a hurdle to answered prayer when it is misapplied. There are blessings God wants to give us in this life, in the present day. If we think they are all in the future, we will not exercise our faith to see their fulfillment in our lives *now*. Where faith is not applied, fulfillment cannot be given.

Believers who have this perspective will receive the future blessings for which they have hope and faith, but they will miss out on the blessings God wants to give them today. For example, when you ask God to meet your need to pay next month's mortgage, you don't need the money at a future time. You need it now. That requires faith, not hope.

Second, there is a type of hope that is really just wishful thinking. It is not based on faith, as biblical hope is. Instead, it is based on uncertainty or doubt. We can think of the difference in this way: the first is hope; the second is "hoping." Hoping is when we say: "I hope this happens." "I hope this works." "I hope God hears my prayers."

Wishful thinking is a destructive element in prayer.

Wishful thinking is a destructive element in the present-tense life and practice of prayer. Hebrews 11:1 says, *"Now faith is being **sure** of what we hope for and **certain** of what we do not see"* (emphasis added). As we learned in earlier chapters, we receive what God has promised us *when* we pray. Having faith means speaking and affirming this fact until the answer manifests. Hoping is dangerous because it can cancel our prayers. For example, suppose you ask God for something according to His Word, and you say, "Lord, I believe." Then you get up from your prayer time and say, "Well, I hope it happens." You have just nullified your prayer.

When you pray for a present-day blessing, hope doesn't play a part, except in your confident expectation that what you asked for is on its way. When Daniel continued to pray, even though his answer didn't arrive for three weeks, he was not hoping for an answer; he was waiting for an answer. There's a difference. Suppose you call a friend and say, "I'm making a cake, and I ran out of butter. Would you bring some over?" You're making a request. Your friend says, "I'm on the way." Are you hoping to receive butter? No. You continue preparing the cake because you believe the butter is coming. You're expecting it because your friend has promised to bring it.

The only difficulty with this analogy is the person who promised it. The Bible says, "If God said it, He will do it. If He promised it, He will bring it to pass." (See Numbers 23:19.) But your friend might get detoured, have a flat tire, or change his or her mind. That's why the Bible says, "Don't put your trust in man, but in God." (See Psalm 118:8.)

Hoping doesn't get anything accomplished. How long have you been hoping to go to school, take an evening class, learn computers? Perhaps two years, five years, ten years—and you still haven't done it. How long have you been hoping to lose weight, even though you haven't started a weight-loss program? How long have you been hoping to get a different job, even though you've never filled out any applications? Faith makes you work. Hoping doesn't. Another term for hoping is "Someday I'll...." How long have you been on "Someday Island"?

God's blessings have already been accomplished in the spiritual realm. He is waiting for a human to believe Him so He can release them. If you want to go to college but you don't have any money, take that request to God and say, "God, You said the righteous will be *'like a tree planted by streams of water, which yields its fruit in season and whose leaf does not wither. Whatever he does prospers'* (Ps. 1:3). I'm obeying your Word. I expect to prosper. I will not be *'like chaff that the wind blows away'* (v. 4). I'm going to college because I am the righteous, and my fruit shall come in season." When you're finished, start filling out applications. Otherwise, going to college will only be a hope and a dream.

When we exhibit wishful thinking and doubt, we show that we don't really trust God, that we don't believe Him, that we are skeptical about His character and integrity. Doubt is really an insult to God. No wonder James said that if a person doubts, *"that man should not think he will receive anything from the Lord"* (James 1:7).

Many of us wish and wait. When we don't receive what we asked for, we wonder if God's Word is true. The problem is not with God's Word, but with us. He has already accomplished what we have requested, but we have not been expecting what we asked for. We are not acting as if we have it; therefore, God cannot give it. We're holding Him up. *"The Lord bestows favor and honor; no good thing does he withhold from those whose walk is blameless"* (Ps. 84:11).

5. Praying for Faith

Luke 17:5 says, *"The apostles said to the Lord, 'Increase our faith!'"* Have you ever prayed a prayer like that? You are in good company. The disciples lived with Jesus for over three years. They saw Him cast out demons, heal the sick, and raise the dead, yet they still asked him, *"Increase our faith!"* His answer is wonderful. *"He replied, 'If you have faith as small as a mustard seed, you can say to this mulberry tree, "Be uprooted and planted in the sea," and it will obey you'"* (v. 6).

When I was in Israel, I was shown a mustard tree. It was massive. Then I was shown a mustard seed. It's hard to imagine that such an immense tree can come from such a tiny seed. Jesus was telling His disciples, "You don't need any more faith; just a small amount will move mountains. The little you have can do much, but you aren't using it."

When you pray for faith, you are praying to believe. I don't think you can pray to believe. Either you believe or you don't believe. Such a prayer is really based on unbelief, and therefore it will not be answered. I have never heard of anyone having his faith increased by praying for it. Faith grows as the Word is taken into our lives and acted upon. Romans 10:17 says, *"Faith comes from hearing the message, and the message is heard through the word of Christ."* Faith comes and increases as we hear and believe the Word and put it into practice.

It is not the size of your faith that counts—it is the size of your God. If you believe, you activate heaven. Perhaps you are thinking, "I'm not sure I have faith."

It's not the size of your faith that counts—it's the size of your God. *"Faith comes from hearing...the word of Christ."* If you want to increase your faith, increase your intake of the Word of God. What you know of the Word becomes the limit of your faith because you can believe only what you know. This is why it is very important to belong to a local body of believers where the teaching is well-rounded and covers all aspects of the Christian life. We need to understand how God operates in every area of life because we want to have faith in all those areas. Jesus said, *"According to your faith will it be done to you"* (Matt. 9:29).

6. CARES OF THE WORLD/LAZINESS

There is one last hurdle I want to mention: Neglecting prayer altogether, either through sheer laziness or because of life's busyness and distractions. Laziness and neglect are the worst reasons for not praying. None of us wants to be called a *"wicked, lazy servant"* (Matt. 25:26) by God in regard to this crucial purpose for our lives.

In the parable of the sower, Jesus said, *"The one who received the seed that fell among the thorns is the man who hears the word, but the worries of this life and the deceitfulness of wealth choke it, making it unfruitful"* (Matt. 13:22). When a person doesn't want to bother with prayer because he feels he has more important things to do, or when he allows the many concerns of this life to crowd out the practice of prayer, then whatever he does know about prayer will not bear any fruit in his life.

Matthew 3:10 says, *"The ax is already at the root of the trees, and every tree that does not produce good fruit will be cut down and thrown into the fire."* We must be careful not to become complacent in our knowledge of the Word and neglect to nurture it. However, when we hear, absorb, and apply the Word, we will bear the fruit of much spiritual growth and answered prayer. We will see God's original purposes for blessing the earth fulfilled through our very lives.

Hurdles to Answered Prayer

LET'S PRAY TOGETHER

Heavenly Father,

Your Word says, *"Be self-controlled and alert. Your enemy the devil prowls around like a roaring lion looking for someone to devour. Resist him, standing firm in the faith"* (1 Pet. 5:8–9). We ask You to help us remain alert to the hurdles in our lives that the enemy wants to use to destroy our prayer potential. Help us to resist him as we stand firm in our faith. Let Your Holy Spirit show us where we are being deceived in our attitudes toward prayer and the Word so we can understand and practice true and effective prayer. We ask these things in the name of Jesus, who resisted the enemy through the power of Your Word. Amen.

PUTTING PRAYER INTO PRACTICE

Ask yourself:

- Which of these hurdles best describes my practice of prayer and reading the Word?
- What attitude or outlook do I need to repent from in order to rise above this hurdle through God's grace?

Action Steps:

- Choose one hurdle that represents your current practice of prayer. Consciously take steps to correct it by applying the truth of God's Word to it.
- Each day, as you read the Bible, ask God to open the eyes of your heart to see what He is saying to you through His Word. Practice meditation by spending time thinking about the implications and applications of what you have read.
- After church this week, spend at least five minutes sitting quietly, reflecting on the message and what God is saying to you through it.

Principles

Six hurdles to answered prayer are—

1. *Learning about Prayer but Not Practicing It:* We gain a false sense of satisfaction when we learn about the Bible and prayer but don't actually live out what we have learned. It doesn't matter how much we know; our knowledge will not help us spiritually unless we put it into practice. The best approach to prayer is *to pray.*

2. *Mental Assent rather than Action:* Mental assent *agrees* with God but does not *believe* God. A variation of mental assent is "sense knowledge." This attitude says, "I'll believe it when I see it," whereas faith is believing *before* we see the manifestation of our prayers. James 1:22 tells us that if we think just listening to the Word is enough, we are deceived. We must believe the Word and act on it.

3. *Hearing the Word but Not Absorbing It:* When we don't absorb the Word, Satan steals it away so that it cannot have an impact on our relationship with God. We absorb the Word by meditating on it, by letting it sink into our spirits. When this happens, the devil can't stop the Word because God now has something He can use to accomplish His will in our lives.

4. *Hoping rather than Having Faith:* There are two ways in which the idea of hope can interfere with what God wants to accomplish through prayer: (1) when we apply the biblical definition of hope (future fulfillment) to present-day faith situations; and (2) when our hope is not the biblical kind, but is really just wishful thinking.

5. *Praying for Faith:* When we pray for faith, we are praying to believe. Either we believe or we don't believe. Such a prayer is really based on unbelief and therefore will not be answered. Faith comes and increases as we hear, believe, and obey the Word.

6. *Laziness/Cares of the World:* If we are too lazy to pray, we risk being called a *"wicked, lazy servant"* (Matt. 25:26) by God in regard to this crucial purpose for our lives. When we allow the concerns of this life to crowd out the practice of prayer, then what we do know about prayer will not bear fruit in our lives.

Chapter Nine

Hindrances to Answered Prayer

Clearing out hindrances in our lives will enable us to live in harmony with God and others and to have confidence in prayer.

I n addition to the hurdles described in the last chapter, there are spiritual and emotional hindrances to prayer that we need to address if we are to have true fellowship with God and receive answers to our prayers. Some of these hindrances have been discussed in other places and contexts in this book. However, I have included them in a more systematic way here so we can recognize and understand the major obstacles that hinder our prayers and, therefore, deal with them more effectively.

1. SIN

First, we must acknowledge the impact of sin in our lives. Sin, as the Bible says, *"is so prevalent"* (James 1:21), and our fallen nature causes many problems and misunderstandings in regard to our faith, obedience, and prayers. *"Therefore, get rid of all moral filth and the evil that is so prevalent and humbly accept the word planted in you, which can save you. Do not merely listen to the word, and so deceive yourselves. Do what it says"* (vv. 21–22).

When there is sin—especially willful sin—in your life, and you are not obeying the Word, God will not hear you. You will not receive His favor. Isaiah 59:2 tells us, *"Your iniquities have separated you from your God; your sins have hidden his face from you, so that he will not hear,"* and Psalm 66:18 says, *"If I regard iniquity in my heart, the Lord will not hear me"* (KJV). First John 3:22 says, *"And whatever we ask we receive from Him, because we **keep His commandments and do those things that are pleasing in His sight"*** (NKJV, emphasis added).

However, when we sin, 1 John 2:1 assures us, *"If anybody does sin, we have one who speaks to the Father in our defense—Jesus Christ, the Righteous One."* Scripture also promises us:

> *If my people, who are called by my name, will humble themselves and pray and seek my face and turn from their wicked ways, **then will I hear from heaven** and will forgive their sin and will heal their land.*
> (2 Chron. 7:14, emphasis added)

2. FEAR

Second, fear is a significant hindrance for us to overcome because it often keeps us from believing we can approach God in prayer. First John 4:18 says, *"There is no fear in love. But perfect love drives out fear, because fear has to do with punishment [*"because fear involves torment"* NKJV]. The one who fears is not made perfect in love."* The idea of *"punishment"* in this verse refers to our being afraid to approach God because we think He might remember a sin or failure on our part. It hinders us from having freedom and confidence when we pray. We're afraid to ask God for anything because we believe He has something against us. This kind of fear will block your faith, and, thus, your prayers will be ineffective.

Fear is faith in what could go wrong rather than faith in what could go right.

The Bible says that *"fear involves torment."* Fear immobilizes you. It drains the energy from your body. It is worry without profit. It is faith in what could go wrong rather than faith in what could go right. It is believing what the devil is telling you and what other people are telling you rather than what God is saying to you.

When you go before God, it doesn't matter what your past was like, what you did yesterday, or even what you did this morning that was unpleasing to Him. If you confess your sin before God, appropriating the cleansing blood of Jesus to purify you from all unrighteousness (see 1 John 1:9), then He will forgive you, and you can approach Him as if you had never sinned. No fear needs to be involved in your prayers.

Let's look again at 1 John 4:18: *"The one who fears is not made perfect in love."* Now look at verse nineteen: *"We love because he first loved us."* Verse nineteen has the solution to our fear, to our not being *"made perfect in love."* When we realize that God loved us first and desired a relationship with us even when we didn't know Him and were living in sin, we will understand that we can freely come to Him and ask for forgiveness. Romans 5:8 echoes this idea: *"But God demonstrates his own love for us in this: **while we were still sinners,** Christ died for us"* (emphasis added).

Some believers feel, "That's fine for those who are coming to Christ for the first time, but I've been a Christian for years. The fact that I still sin makes me feel like a failure. How can God forgive me again and again?" Actually, now that you are a believer, you are in an even better position. Look at Romans 5:9: *"Since we have now been justified by his blood, how much more shall we be saved from God's wrath through him!"* We have Jesus' word that we will continue to be forgiven. When Jesus told Peter that he should continue to forgive someone, no matter how many times the person sinned against him (see Matthew 18:21–22), He was reflecting God's attitude toward forgiveness. Isaiah 43:25 says, *"I, even I, am he who blots out your transgressions, for my own sake, and remembers your sins no more."* Be encouraged! God wants you to live with the assurance of forgiveness and move forward in His purposes with confidence. *"For God has not given us a spirit of fear, but of power and of love and of a sound mind"* (2 Tim. 1:7 NKJV).

3. Guilt

Guilt is related to the fear of not being forgiven. Some people live with a constant sense of being condemned by God; therefore, they always feel guilty. However, Romans

8:1–2 tells us, *"Therefore, there is now no condemnation for those who are in Christ Jesus, because through Christ Jesus the law of the Spirit of life set me free from the law of sin and* [its consequence] *death."*

"There is now no condemnation" (Rom. 8:1). This truth is crucial for us to understand if we are to approach God in prayer. I remember speaking at a prayer meeting about the freedom from condemnation that we have in Christ. After the meeting, someone came up to me and said, "That word was so important for me; I thought that because I'd done some terrible things in my life, God wasn't going to use me anymore. I felt as if God wouldn't want me to be a part of His work any longer." Even after some people have been forgiven, they may go to church, worship, sing, and seem happy, but inside they still feel guilty about things they did in the past. Their spiritual growth is stunted because they think God is holding their sins against them, and they no longer approach Him in faith and perfect love. This person said, "I asked for forgiveness, but I just needed to hear God say, 'It's okay. You're forgiven.'"

> **If God says He has forgotten your sins, then He has forgotten them.**

God has forgiven and forgotten your sin if you have confessed it, repented of it, and believed that it is covered by the blood of Jesus. Hebrews 8:12 says, *"For I will forgive their wickedness and will remember their sins no more."*

Suppose you are in a prayer meeting or worship service, and you begin to remember things you've done wrong in the past—things for which you've already been forgiven and cleansed, but which continue to make you feel guilty. Why do you feel this way? Sometimes guilt comes from distrust. If you have asked God to forgive you, He has forgiven you. If you are still carrying the sin around in your heart and mind, then you are doubting that God forgave you. That is why the guilt comes back to life. The devil uses that guilt to undermine your faith; when you pray, your faith is weak, and so your prayers aren't answered.

The Bible says, "[God] *will tread our sins underfoot and hurl all our iniquities into the depths of the sea"* (Mic. 7:19), and *"I, even I, am he who blots out your transgressions, for my own sake, and remembers your sins no more"* (Isa. 43:25). God chooses not to remember your sins once they have been forgiven. He does not allow them to stand in the way of your relationship with Him. Here's what's important about this fact: Since He has chosen to forget them, He doesn't want you to remind Him about them either. Don't bring up old baggage when God doesn't know what you're talking about. God is so powerful that, if He told you He has forgotten your sins, then He has forgotten them. If He has already decided to forget them, then He doesn't remember them. What a blessing!

One of my college professors used to say, "After we ask for forgiveness, God puts up a little sign that says, 'No fishing.'" He has cast our sins into the sea of forgetfulness, and we aren't to go fishing there. We say, "But, Lord, remember what I did a couple of years ago? That is still on my mind." God says, "I don't know what you're talking about. I forgave you. I forgot about it." Thank God that everything in the past is forgiven and forgotten. We have been cleansed from it.

If you are burdened with guilt about your past, you can walk into God's presence without feeling condemned. There is no condemnation for those who are in Christ Jesus because God has forgiven you through Christ. Hebrews 10:14 says, *"By one sacrifice* [Christ] **has made perfect forever** *those who are* **being made holy**" (emphasis added). Christ has already made you perfect in Him through His sacrifice on the cross, yet you are also in a process of *"being made holy."*

If you have sin in your life right now, put it under the blood of Jesus. Let Him cast your sin in that sea of forgetfulness so you can have power in prayer with God. Seek reconciliation in your broken relationships and restitution for wrongs you have committed, as God leads. If you sin in the future, ask God to forgive you and to continue the process of sanctification in your life. Accept His forgiveness and draw near to Him again in confident faith:

> *"This is the covenant I will make with them after that time, says the Lord. I will put my laws in their hearts, and I will write them on their minds." Then he adds:*

"Their sins and lawless acts I will remember no more."
And where these have been forgiven, there is no longer
any sacrifice for sin. Therefore, brothers, since we have
confidence to enter the Most Holy Place by the blood
of Jesus, by a new and living way opened for us
through the curtain, that is, his body, and since we
have a great priest over the house of God, let us draw
near to God with a sincere heart in full assurance of
faith, having our hearts sprinkled to cleanse us from a
guilty conscience and having our bodies washed with
pure water.   (Heb. 10:16–22)

4. FEELINGS OF INFERIORITY

Some people are hindered in prayer because they don't
believe they are worthy enough to receive an answer. When
you have a low opinion of yourself, it
is because you do not know God's
true opinion of you, which He reveals
in His Word. This is a crucial hurdle
to overcome so that it will not sabotage your prayer life. You cannot pray
effectively if you are ashamed of yourself and do not consider yourself
worthy to receive what you are asking God for.

A low opinion of yourself is not from God. You are very valuable to Him.

The first chapter of Ephesians is a marvelous passage
that describes how God truly feels about us. It was a special blessing to me when I was a teenager.

In love [God] **predestined us to be adopted as his**
sons *through Jesus Christ, in accordance with his*
pleasure and will—to the praise of his glorious grace,
which he has freely given us in the One he loves. In
him we have redemption through his blood, the for-
giveness of sins, in accordance with the riches of
God's grace that he lavished on us with all wisdom
and understanding. And he made known to us the
mystery of his will according to his good pleasure,
which he purposed in Christ, to be put into effect
when the times will have reached their fulfillment—to
bring all things in heaven and on earth together under
one head, even Christ. In him we were also **chosen.**

(vv. 4–11, emphasis added)

170

We were chosen in Christ long before the earth was made. God loves you so much that He has lavished His love on you. A low opinion of yourself or self-hatred is not from God, but from the enemy. He uses these things as an insult to God. He doesn't want you to realize that if God loved you so much that He gave you the best He had, then your value to Him must be incalculable.

The entire chapter of Hebrews 10 tells us how precious we are to God. It talks about the fact that Jesus our Substitute became the sacrifice, or propitiation, for our sin. He redeemed our lives. The result is that *"we [can] have confidence to enter the Most Holy Place by the blood of Jesus"* (v. 19). This thought is also found in Hebrews 4:16: *"Let us then approach the throne of grace with confidence ["come boldly to the throne of grace" NKJV], so that we may receive mercy and find grace to help us in our time of need."* In light of our value to God, we can treat ourselves with respect and approach Him as a chosen child who has been given *"the riches of God's grace"* (Eph. 1:7).

Thus, the way a person feels about himself plays a significant role in how he approaches God in prayer. Many are not having their prayers answered because they don't believe they deserve an answer. However, when you have the right estimation of yourself as a redeemed child of God, you don't come to prayer as someone who is begging. Instead, you confidently present your case. Prayer is not trying to get God to do something for you by making Him feel sorry for you. It is coming to Him knowing that you not only deserve what you ask because of the righteousness of Christ, but you also have a right to it because it is based on His Word.

You need to present the evidence of His Word as in a court of law. In addition, you must believe that when you walk into the courtroom of Jehovah, Jesus is on your left, which is the witness side. (See Hebrews 7:25.) The Holy Spirit is on your right side because He serves as your counsel. (See, for example, John 14:16–17.) What is wonderful about coming into God's courtroom to plead your case is that the Judge is your heavenly Father, the witness is your Elder Brother, and the Holy Spirit is your personal counselor. How can you lose the case?

Jesus goes before the Father and testifies to your faith in Him. When you don't know how to plead correctly, the Holy Spirit helps you in your weakness. When you aren't sure how to quote the promises, He helps you with groanings that cannot be expressed. (See Romans 8:26–27.) He speaks to God directly from the heart of a legal counsel. Therefore, when your efforts are inadequate, you have assistance to help you pray.

Some people believe that they shouldn't act boldly when they pray. Instead, they are mild-mannered and fawning in prayer, mistakenly believing that God will see them as humble and grant their requests. We need to understand the true nature of humility. Humility doesn't mean trying to be something you're not. A humble person is, first of all, a person who knows who he is. He is a person who is honest. However, you can't *be* who you are if you don't *know* who you are. That is why, if you don't know who you are, it's difficult to approach God in prayer. We must realize we are not fallen angels who cannot be redeemed. We are not even righteous angels who are servants in God's house. We are God's own children, and we need to approach Him as His children.

You can't *be* who you are if you don't *know* who you are. You are God's own child.

How would you feel if your child came into the house crawling on the floor because he was afraid to look at you, and said, "Would you please feed me today?" That would be an affront to your love, wouldn't it? Something is wrong if your child is afraid to face you and ask for food. If you are a child of God, then you are to walk boldly into the throne room and say, "Hello, Abba." Your Father will say, "What can I do for you, My child? Remind Me of what I promised you." And then you present your case.

If you were in a court of law, and your lawyer were presenting your case for you, would your attorney stand there and merely say, "Judge, please, please, let him go. I plead with you to let him go." Pleading your case doesn't mean saying, "O God, *please* forgive me!" It means telling God, for example, "According to Your Word, You have said, '*This righteousness from God comes through faith in Jesus Christ to all who believe'* (Rom. 3:22), and I'm presenting Your words as evidence. I believe; therefore, I'm asking that You justify me." You can't pray like that if you feel afraid and inferior.

I'm going to use an old case study to show you how most people pray. Jesus told the story of a man who left his father's house. He went off and made a mess of his life until he had nothing left—financially, physically, emotionally, or spiritually. Finally, he said, "I will go home to my father, and I will ask him to make me one of his hired servants." The man had inferiority problems. He had no idea how much his father loved and valued him. When he arrived home, his father was so excited that he told his servants to kill the fatted calf for a feast, to put a new robe on his son, and to place the ring of authority on his son's finger. He restored his son to his place in the family. Before the son could say what he had planned to say, which was, "Father, I am unworthy to be called your son," the father joyfully said, "My son who was lost is found!" (See Luke 15:11–24.)

Who cooked the fatted calf for the boy and took care of his other needs? The servants did, acting on the orders of the father. Most of us don't understand what prayer signifies about our relationship with God. The parable of the prodigal son illustrates this relationship for us. When we go to God in prayer, we are supposed to do so recognizing who He says we are. All who are in Christ Jesus are children of God. Who are the servants? They are His angels. *"In speaking of the angels he says, 'He makes his angels winds, his servants flames of fire'"* (Heb. 1:7). God is saying to each of us, in effect, "You aren't a servant; you are a son. Your prayers activate angels, who minister under My authority." Too often we come to prayer and say, "Lord, I am Your unworthy servant." God responds, "What are you talking about? You are My beloved child!"

When Jesus was tempted by the devil, He responded strongly by using God's Word: *"It is written, 'Man does not live on bread alone, but on every word that comes from the mouth of God'"* (Matt. 4:4). *"It is written: 'Worship the Lord your God, and serve him only'"* (v. 10). The Bible says that after Jesus' temptation, *"angels came and attended him"*

(v. 11). When you pray like a son, you activate angels, and they go about fulfilling what you prayed, according to the Word. *"Are not all angels ministering spirits sent to serve those who will inherit salvation?"* (Heb. 1:14).

When you pray, keep in mind who you are in Christ and what God has promised you. If you do not immediately receive an answer, be careful not to allow feelings of un-worthiness to cause you to think, "I'm not sure anything happened." It happened. It may take a week. It may take twenty-one days, as in the case of Daniel. It may take longer. However, your prayer has been answered and will be manifested. Believe me, friends, God heard what you said. It's on record. Angels are already watching. Everything you pray in accordance with the Word begins to change things.

Remember—you are not a servant, but a child of God. *"He has made us accepted in the Beloved"* (Eph. 1:6 NKJV). God loved you before the foundation of the earth. When you were estranged from Him by sin, He sent His Son to die for you. He has made you worthy in Christ Jesus. He has made you a coheir with His Son. He sends His angels to minister to you. Therefore, live and pray accordingly.

5. DOUBT

If any of you lacks wisdom, he should ask God, who gives generously to all without finding fault, and it will be given to him. But when he asks, he must be-lieve and not doubt, because he who doubts is like a wave of the sea, blown and tossed by the wind. That man should not think he will receive anything from the Lord; he is a double-minded man, unstable in all he does. (James 1:5–8)

Although we have covered the topic of doubt in other sections of this book, it is such a major hindrance to prayer that we should briefly review it here. Doubt is making a big fuss before God about what you want Him to do, and then, when the prayer is over, not believing a word you said. It is being in a prayer meeting and saying, "God, I believe You," and then leaving the meeting muttering, "I'm not sure about what we prayed in there." You show that you don't believe when you don't expect the answer, when you don't make arrangements for the answer.

For example, if you are praying for someone in your family to become saved, you can buy a Bible for that person ahead of time. That's believing. If you are praying for somebody to be healed, you can arrange to take the person out to eat. Tell the person, "I'm inviting you out to dinner." "Why?" "I prayed for you to be healed; I expect you to be healed. I'm making arrangements. When you get to the point that God manifests your healing, I'm going to take you out to dinner."

Trust the generosity and kindness of God, putting your faith in His character and Word.

The Scriptures tell us that we must believe. *"Let him ask of God, who gives to all liberally and without reproach, and it will be given to him. But let him ask in faith, with no doubting"* (vv. 5–6 NKJV). Instead of doubting, let us trust the generosity and kindness of God, putting our faith in His character and Word.

6. WRONG MOTIVES

The Bible says that if your motives are wrong, your prayers will be hindered. *"When you ask, you do not receive, because you ask with wrong motives* ["ask amiss" NKJV], *that you may spend what you get on your pleasures"* (James 4:3). What are your motives for praying? Are you asking God for something just so you can promote your own ego or for other selfish purposes? Or are you asking God to fulfill His Word so that His kingdom can come on the earth?

God knows we have needs, and it's not wrong to request that He fulfill them based on His Word. Jesus said, *"Your Father knows what you need before you ask him"* (Matt. 6:8). Yet our main focus should be honoring God and promoting His purposes. When we have our priorities right, we can trust Him to meet our daily needs. Jesus promised us,

Do not worry, saying, "What shall we eat?" or "What shall we drink?" or "What shall we wear?" For the

pagans run after all these things, and your heavenly Father knows that you need them. But seek first his kingdom and his righteousness, and all these things will be given to you as well." (vv. 31–33)

Therefore, when you pray, check your reasons for praying. Ask God to forgive you for any wrong motives you may have and to enable you to develop the right motives through the work of the Holy Spirit in your life. *"For it is God who works in you to will and to act according to his good purpose"* (Phil. 2:13).

7. BITTERNESS

Bitterness is a dangerous thing, especially in regard to prayer. It often indicates a hidden hatred. Bitterness means

Bitterness goes to the very source of your life and dries it up.

you are holding something against someone and not releasing that person through forgiveness. You hurt yourself more than the person against whom you are bitter. When you hold onto bitterness, it goes to the very source of your life and dries it up. Not only will you be affected spiritually, but you will also begin to wither mentally, socially, and physically. It is like a cancer. We should reserve our hatred for the devil alone.

How does bitterness affect your prayer life? The Bible says, *"If I regard iniquity in my heart, the Lord will not hear me"* (Ps. 66:18 KJV). Bitterness is iniquity. God hates iniquity more than sin, if a distinction between the two is possible. Iniquity is a special kind of sin. The Hebrew word for iniquity is *avon.* It means perversity or moral evil. Any rebellion against God is considered sin. However, iniquity is a vicious kind of sin that God specifically says He hates. In Hebrews 1:9, we read, *"Thou hast loved righteousness, and hated iniquity"* (KJV). The Greek word for *"iniquity"* in this verse is *anomia,* which means lawlessness or an offense against the law.

Iniquity is a secret sin—not in the sense that you go off somewhere to commit it, but in the sense that it is something you can't see, such as jealousy. For example, it is when you smile at someone, but you're really envious of what that person has. Or when you hug somebody during a church service and say, "God bless you," but you really despise the person. That's iniquity. God says He hates that kind of sin more than any other. Therefore, He says that if we willfully hold such things in our hearts, it doesn't matter how long we pray; He won't hear us.

Bitterness is an especially hideous, dangerous sin. *"See to it that no one misses the grace of God and that no bitter root grows up to cause trouble and defile many"* (Heb. 12:15). To guard against this sin and keep our prayers from being hindered, we need to maintain transparent, pure hearts before God and man. *"Let all bitterness, wrath, anger, clamor, and evil speaking be put away from you, with all malice. And be kind to one another, tenderhearted, forgiving one another, just as God in Christ forgave you"* (Eph. 4:31–32 NKJV).

8. UNFORGIVENESS

Like bitterness, unforgiveness will hinder your prayers by blocking your relationships with God and other people. Mark 11:25 says, *"And when you stand praying, if you hold anything against anyone, forgive him, so that your Father in heaven may forgive you your sins."*

Unforgiveness can be an underlying presence in our lives, even when we don't realize we're harboring it in our hearts. Have you forgiven your ex-wife, ex-husband, boyfriend, or whoever it is that makes you angry every time you think about him or her? How about a member of the church who hurt you or a friend who owes you money? How about someone on the job who wronged you—someone you're still mad at after three weeks, six months, or even ten years? These things can block your prayer life because you are nurturing an unforgiving spirit. The Bible says, *"'In your anger do not sin': Do not let the sun go down while you are still angry, and do not give the devil a foothold"* (Eph. 4:26–27). Unforgiveness does not reflect the character of Christ, and it demonstrates ingratitude for the vast forgiveness God has extended to you. Jesus made this point very clear in the parable of the unforgiving servant in Matthew 18:23–35. You need to resolve issues of unforgiveness in your life if you want God to hear your prayers.

9. Broken Family Relationships

Broken relationships in the home, between a husband and wife, for example, will also hinder your prayers. First Peter 3:7 says, *"Husbands, in the same way be considerate as you live with your wives, and treat them with respect as the weaker partner and as heirs with you of the gracious gift of life, so that nothing will hinder your prayers."* Peter was saying, "Husbands, dwell with your wives with understanding, and don't let there be any animosity between you, lest your prayers be hindered."

Although he was speaking specifically to husbands, the same principle may be applied to relationships between any family members, since the law of unforgiveness applies to everyone. As believers, the Spirit of God dwells within us. Therefore, we are to demonstrate the nature of God to one another. Psalm 103:8–10 tells us, *"The Lord is compassionate and gracious, slow to anger, abounding in love. He will not always accuse, nor will he harbor his anger forever; he does not treat us as our sins deserve or repay us according to our iniquities."* If we do not demonstrate the love, compassion, forgiveness, and grace of God to others, we are misrepresenting Him. How can we ask Him to fulfill His purposes by answering our prayers when we are violating those very purposes by the way we treat others?

Matthew 5:23–24 says,

> *If you are offering your gift at the altar and there remember that your brother has something against you, leave your gift there in front of the altar. First go and be reconciled to your brother; then come and offer your gift.*

If there are broken or hurting relationships in your home, God is saying, in effect, "Don't come to church to pray. Stay home and reconcile before you come." If you try to worship and praise while ignoring the fact that your relationships are strained or estranged, you're going to end up wasting your time before God. Put those relationships right, and then go worship and pray. Also, if you are in a worship service or prayer meeting and God shows you a relationship that needs to be mended, yield to the Holy Spirit's prompting and make things right as soon as you can. *"If it is possible, as far as it depends on you, live at peace with everyone"* (Rom. 12:17–18).

10. IDOLS

*"Son of man, these men have set up idols in their hearts and put wicked stumbling blocks before their faces. **Should I let them inquire of me at all**?"* (Ezek. 14:3, emphasis added). In this sobering verse, God is saying, "I will not answer your prayers if you are seeking idols." He is not speaking of statues. He is referring to idols of the heart. We must be careful not to set up idols in our lives, however subtle they may be.

Cable television can be an idol. Your car can be an idol. Clothes can be idols. Your wife and children can be idols. A boyfriend or girlfriend can be an idol. Your reputation can be an idol. An idol is anything we give higher priority than God.

The displacement of God from His rightful position in our lives can be gradual. It can happen without our realizing it. We need to examine our lives to see what is most important to us, what our priorities are, and how we are spending our time. God deserves our primary love, respect, and devotion. *"Love the LORD your God with all your heart and with all your soul and with all your strength"* (Deut. 6:5).

11. STINGINESS

Finally, an ungenerous heart can hinder your prayers. Proverbs 21:13 says, *"If a man shuts his ears to the cry of the poor, he too will cry out and not be answered."* God is telling us that if we are stingy, it can prevent our prayers from being heard. How can we ask God to provide for our needs when we're not concerned about the needs of those who are less fortunate than we are? However, if we are compassionate and generous, if we are givers, we can be assured that our prayers will be answered. *"A generous man will prosper; he who refreshes others will himself be refreshed"* (Prov. 11:25). *"A generous man will himself be blessed, for he shares his food with the poor"* (Prov. 22:9).

In addition, when we are generous toward God, He promises to provide for us abundantly:

> *"Bring the whole tithe into the storehouse, that there may be food in my house. Test me in this,"* says the LORD Almighty, *"and see if I will not throw open the floodgates of heaven and pour out so much blessing that you will not have room enough for it."* (Mal. 3:10)

THROW OFF YOUR HINDRANCES

Hebrews 12:1 says, *"Let us throw off ["lay aside" NKJV] everything that hinders and the sin that so easily entangles, and let us run with perseverance the race marked out for us."* Let us determine, through God's grace, to remove these hindrances from our lives so we can live in harmony with God and others, and have confidence and effectiveness in prayer.

LET'S PRAY TOGETHER

Heavenly Father,

As Your Word says, we are burdened by things that hinder us spiritually and emotionally, and we too easily become entangled with sin. These encumbrances keep us from having a joyful, unbroken relationship with You and with our families, friends, coworkers, and others. We ask You to enable us to have a true understanding of who we are in Your Son, Jesus Christ. Help us to clear away each of the hindrances in our lives so we can live freely as Your children and so we can pray in harmony with Your will and purposes for the world. We ask this in the name of Jesus, who is our Burden-Bearer—who has carried our sins and sorrows, who has healed us by His own wounds, and whose suffering on our behalf has brought us peace with You (Isa. 53:4–5). Amen.

PUTTING PRAYER INTO PRACTICE

Ask yourself:

- Is there anything in my life that is keeping me from a clear conscience and unbroken fellowship with God?
- Have I confessed my sins to God and asked His forgiveness?
- Have I accepted the forgiveness of God? Or am I still holding onto past sins and guilt?
- Have I recognized that I am a child of God? Have I thought about what my relationship with God really means?
- What are my motives when I pray?
- Am I harboring bitterness or unforgiveness against anyone?

Action Steps:

- If you find yourself beginning to doubt after you have prayed, consciously replace those doubts with what the Word of God says about your situation.
- If there are relationships in your life that need mending, ask God to help you let go of any bitterness. Take a step this week to repair one of those relationships by forgiving someone or asking for forgiveness.
- Write down anything you think you are putting ahead of God in your life, such as money, a relationship, or your career. Offer it to God and begin to renew your love and commitment to Him this week by spending extra time worshipping Him and acknowledging His Fatherhood and His sovereignty in your life.

Principles

Major hindrances to prayer are—

1. *Sin:* If we humble ourselves, seek God, and turn from sin, God will forgive us and hear our prayers (2 Chron. 7:14).

2. *Fear:* Fear blocks our prayers by undermining our faith. We must accept God's forgiveness and the new spirit He has given us—one of power, love, and a sound mind.

3. *Guilt:* To be free from feelings of condemnation, we must realize that God not only has *forgiven* us, but has also *forgotten* our sins; therefore, we can pray with a clean conscience and with assurance.

4. *Feelings of Inferiority:* As God's beloved children, we are not beggars in prayer. We can pray confidently based on God's Word, Jesus' testimony, and the Spirit's advocacy.

5. *Doubt:* Doubt hinders our prayers because we don't truly believe what we are saying. We show our trust in God by making arrangements for the fulfillment of our requests.

6. *Wrong Motives:* When we have our priorities right—putting God's kingdom and honor above all else—He will hear our prayers and meet our daily needs.

7. *Bitterness:* God will not hear our prayers if we are holding on to iniquity in our hearts, such as jealousy. We need to maintain transparent, pure hearts before God and man.

8. *Unforgiveness:* Unforgiveness hinders our prayers by blocking our relationships with God and others. Ephesians 4:26–27 says, *"Do not let the sun go down while you are still angry, and do not give the devil a foothold."*

9. *Broken Family Relationships:* God will not answer our prayers if we violate His purposes by failing to demonstrate His love and grace to our family members. We must reconcile broken relationships as soon as we can.

10. *Idols:* We need to examine our priorities. Anything we value more than God is an idol and will hinder our prayers. God deserves our highest love and respect.

11. *Stinginess:* Proverbs 21:13 says, *"If a man shuts his ears to the cry of the poor, he too will cry out and not be answered."* If we are stingy, we won't be heard, but if we are compassionate and generous, our prayers will be answered.

Part IV

The Power of Prayer

Chapter Ten

The Power of the Word

***God wants to use His power in the world. However,
for Him to do so, we must understand how to
appropriate His Word.***

O ver the last several chapters, we've looked at how to
approach God in prayer as well as specific hurdles
and hindrances that keep our prayers from being answered. Once we understand our role as God's mediators
for the world and have dealt with areas in our lives that
block our prayers, we need to make sure we truly understand the power behind prayer: God's Word, the name of
Jesus, and the Holy Spirit. We will explore these themes in
the next few chapters.

In this chapter, we're going to look at the power of the
Word. To fully understand this power, we first need to remind ourselves of what prayer is:

Prayer is earthly license for heavenly interference.

The heart of prayer is asking God to intervene in the
world to fulfill His eternal purposes for mankind. Inter-
woven throughout this book has been the principle that we
are to pray to God on the basis of His Word—the revelation
of who He is, what His will is, and what He has promised.
Remember that when God gave man dominion over the
earth, He gave him the freedom to legally function as its
authority. He placed His will for the earth on the cooperation of the will of man. However, even though man has been
given free will and authority over the earth, this doesn't
mean that he should do anything he wants to with his own

life and with the resources of the world. Neither man nor the world will function properly or fulfill their potential outside of God's will—because they were designed to function in alignment with God's purposes. Just as the creator of a product knows how he has designed that product to function, God knows how we are meant to function and has provided that knowledge in His Word.

Therefore, as we have seen, the key to effective prayer is understanding God's purpose for your life—as a human being in general, and as an individual specifically. In this way, God's will can become the authority of your prayers. True prayer is calling forth what God has already purposed and predestined—the establishment of His plans for the earth. That means that whatever we ask God to do in our lives, in the lives of others, or in the world, must be based on His will. God's purpose is to be both the motivation and the content for our prayers. In other words—

God's purpose is both the motivation and the content for our prayers.

God's purpose is the "raw material" of prayer.

It is through God's Word that we can know, believe, and agree in faith with God's will. Without His Word, our prayers have no foundation. They are based merely on our opinions, desires, and feelings rather than on *"the living and enduring word of God"* (1 Pet. 1:23). Such prayers are powerless to effect change. However, all the power of God is at the disposal of true prayer. God wants to use His power in the world; however, for Him to do so, we must understand how to appropriate His Word.

Prayer is actually very simple. It is speaking the Word to God exactly as He gave it to us. There is no difference between what the people in the Bible were given by God as the basis for their effective prayers and what you and I are given to work with. They relied on what God has given all mankind—His Word.

Our power in prayer is the Word of God. He has already given this to us. Our job is to learn how to handle it properly and responsibly (2 Tim. 2:15). Since we receive the same raw material for prayer that other believers have received, our effectiveness or ineffectiveness in prayer often has to do with how we handle His Word. It is how we use what God has given us that can make the difference between answered and unanswered prayer. [We can use God's Word correctly only when we understand what it is and how to apply it.]

GOD HIMSELF IS SPEAKING IN THE WORD

First, we must understand that God Himself is speaking in the Word, because the Word is who He is: *"In the beginning was the Word, and the Word was with God, and the **Word was God**"* (John 1:1, emphasis added). Therefore, God's presence becomes a part of our prayers when we speak His Word in faith.]

In 1 Kings 19, we read that Elijah did not find God in the wind, earthquake, or fire, but in *"a still small voice"* (v. 12). While many people want to see a manifestation of God's power, they fail to realize that His Word is the foundation of that power—*that the power is only a reflection of the greatness of God Himself.* It was His *"still small voice"* that was behind the forces of nature that Elijah saw. The power of God's Word is so great that if our faith is the size of a mustard seed, mountains can be moved. (See Matthew 17:20.)

THE WORD REVEALS GOD'S NATURE

Next, the Word reveals God's nature—and it is His nature that reflects His will. Everything God says is a revelation of His character and purposes. Again, He and His Word cannot be separated. That is why God's fulfillment of His Word is a matter of personal integrity for Him.

The question for us is this: How will we respond to what the Word reveals about God's character? Numbers 23:19 says, *"God is not a man, that he should lie, nor a son of man, that he should change his mind. Does he speak and then not act? Does he promise and not fulfill?"* Do we believe that God is honorable and that He will keep His Word? A cardinal principle of answered prayer is belief in the trustworthiness of the One to whom you're praying. The power of your prayers depends on it. The Word will work in your life only as you believe it:

> *And we also thank God continually because, when you received the word of God, which you heard from us, you accepted it not as the word of men, but as it actually is, the word of God, **which is at work in you who believe**.* (1 Thess. 2:13, emphasis added)

You demonstrate that you believe someone when you show confidence in his word and character. However, if you do not believe him, you reveal that you do not trust him. The same thing applies in your relationship with God. What do you demonstrate about your belief (or disbelief) in God? If God promises something, but you don't believe it will come to pass, you're telling God, "I have no confidence in You." You may think, "Oh, I would never say that to God!" Yet you might actually be saying that to Him all the time by not believing His Word.

Belief is trust in action.

Your belief is evidence that you trust God. He is not impressed by how many Scriptures you quote or how long you pray. He is moved and convinced when you believe what He has told you, and when you prove it by acting on it. *Belief is trust in action.*

THE WORD IS ALIVE

Moreover, there is power in the Word because it is not just knowledge and facts to us; it is life itself:

> *Take to heart all the words I have solemnly declared to you this day, so that you may command your children to obey carefully all the words of this law. They are not just idle words for you—they are your life.* (Deut. 32:46–47)

> *The Spirit gives life; the flesh counts for nothing. The words I have spoken to you are spirit and they are life.* (John 6:63)

You have been born again, not of perishable seed, but of imperishable, through the living and enduring word of God. For, "All men are like grass, and all their glory is like the flowers of the field; the grass withers and the flowers fall, but the word of the Lord stands forever." And this is the word that was preached to you.
(1 Pet. 1:23–25)

The word of God is living and active. Sharper than any double-edged sword, it penetrates even to dividing soul and spirit, joints and marrow; it judges the thoughts and attitudes of the heart. (Heb. 4:12)

The Word is alive—that's how powerful it is! What did God use to create the world? *"[The Word] was with God in the beginning. Through him all things were made; without him nothing was made that has been made"* (John 1:2–3).

What did God give to Abraham that caused Him to believe? *"Abram fell face down, and **God said to him**, 'As for me, this is my covenant with you: You will be the father of many nations'"* (Gen. 17:3–4, emphasis added).

What did God give to Moses that made him so successful? *"When the LORD saw that he had gone over to look, **God called to him** from within the bush, 'Moses! Moses!' And Moses said, 'Here I am'"* (Exod. 3:4, emphasis added; see also verses 5–10).

What did God give Ezekiel to make him a powerful prophet? Fifty times in the book of Ezekiel, the prophet reported, *"The word of the LORD came to me."* (See, for example, Ezekiel 3:16.)

What did God send to the world to redeem it? *"The Word became flesh and made his dwelling among us. We have seen his glory, the glory of the One and Only, who came from the Father, full of grace and truth"* (John 1:14).

What did Jesus give His disciples for salvation and sanctification? *"Whoever hears my word and believes him who sent me has eternal life and will not be condemned; he has crossed over from death to life"* (John 5:24). *"You are already clean because of the word I have spoken to you"*

(John 15:3). *"Sanctify them by the truth; your word is truth"* (John 17:17).

What did the disciples use to continue Jesus' ministry on earth?

> *"Now, Lord, consider their threats and **enable your servants to speak your word** with great boldness."* *...After they prayed, the place where they were meeting was shaken. And they were all filled with the Holy Spirit and **spoke the word of God boldly**.*
>
> (Acts 4:29, 31, emphasis added)

The Word is alive and active on our behalf. Probably no one quoted Scripture more than Jesus did. When He was tempted by the devil in the wilderness, what did He do? Each time, He gave the devil God's Word, saying, *"It is written"* (Matt. 4:4, 7, 10). Jesus was so well acquainted with the Word that He wasn't fooled by the enemy's distortion of it. (See verse 6.) God watches over His Word to fulfill it (Jer. 1:12). That is why, when Jesus spoke the Word in faith, God fulfilled it, and Christ overcame temptation.

What do we usually do when we are tempted? We say something like, "Devil, I bind you. You have to get away from me. The Lord is stronger than you. Protect me, Lord." Jesus didn't say anything like that. He quoted only the Word. God is a God of the Word. He says, *"[My Word] will not return to me empty, but will accomplish what I desire and achieve the purpose for which I sent it"* (Isa. 55:11). If the church would believe this Scripture, it could shake the world. No Word of God is empty of power. As Jesus said, "Nothing is impossible with God's Word." (See Mark 10:27.)

However, we need to remember that, if we want the Word to work powerfully in our lives, we have to make sure it is inside us. Jesus said, *"If you abide in Me, and My words abide* [are living] *in you, you will ask what you desire, and it shall be done for you"* (John 15:7 NKJV). Perhaps you've read this verse and tried it, but it didn't work. Maybe you don't even bother trying to apply that verse to your life any more; it's just a nice-sounding Scripture to you. Yet Christ was giving us the key to success. What's the first word in the verse? *"If."* We like the *"it shall be done"* part, but we often forget the *"if."*

There are two conditions to answered prayer: *"If you abide in Me,"* and *"If...My words abide in you."* First, what does it mean for you to abide in Jesus? It means to constantly flow in spiritual communion with Him. You do this by fellowshipping with Him and worshipping Him, by praying and fasting.

Second, what does it mean to have His words abiding or living in you? Here is how you can test whether or not the Word is in you: What is the first thing that comes out of your mouth when you are under pressure? Is it an affirmation of faith? Or is it fear, confusion, frustration, doubt, or anger? We know the Word is truly inside us when it directs our thoughts and actions.

God fulfills His Word— not your suggestions or feelings.

You can't get the Word inside of you by keeping it on a shelf in your house. You can't get the Word in your spirit by putting it under your pillow at night and expecting to absorb it by osmosis. You can't even get the Word in you by having someone preach it to you. Preaching only stirs up faith. You have to have the Word in you already. You have to be reading and meditating on the Word regularly.

Jesus gave us the condition, *"If...My words abide in you,"* so the last part of the verse having to do with prayer could be fulfilled in us: *"Ask what you desire, and it shall be done for you."* If His words are in you, then what you desire and ask for will reflect those words. Do you see the connection? If you are filled with the Word, then you won't ask for just anything you feel like. You will ask on the basis of His Word, which is the thing He watches over to fulfill.

Remember that most of our prayers aren't being answered because we are praying for things He never asked us to pray for. However, when we pray according to His Word, we know we are praying the will of God. God performs His Word, and nothing else. He doesn't perform your suggestions or feelings. He doesn't perform your perspective on things. Therefore, if you don't bring Him His Word, you won't be able to experience *"it shall be done for you."* Too often we think the phrase *"ask what you desire"* means we can ask for anything. Yet Christ was saying, in effect, "If My Word is abiding in you, then you can ask for what's abiding in you, and it will be done." That is the power of the Word.

THE WORD BUILDS FAITH

The Word is also powerful because it produces in us the thing that pleases God and causes Him to respond to our requests: *faith.* As we have already seen, God's Word is the parent of all faith. *"Faith comes from hearing the message, and the message is heard through the word of Christ"* (Rom. 10:17). *"By faith we understand that the universe was formed at God's command, so that what is seen was not made out of what was visible"* (Heb. 11:3). Faith is the result of dwelling in and on the Word of God. When the Word of God is lived and practiced in our lives, it becomes power to us.

For the rest of your life, your goal should be to build your faith because the Bible makes it clear that faith is how we live: *"The righteous will live by his faith"* (Hab. 2:4; see also Romans 1:17; Galatians 3:11; Hebrews 10:38). We live by faith, not by sight (2 Cor. 5:7).

> *I have been crucified with Christ and I no longer live, but Christ lives in me. The life I live in the body, I live by faith in the Son of God, who loved me and gave himself for me.* (Gal. 2:20)

You have to work on this thing called faith—faith in God and His Word. Jesus said, *"It is written: 'Man does not live on bread alone, but on every word that comes from the mouth of God'"* (Matt. 4:4). Your faith needs to be fed. It needs to feed on the Word if you are to be spiritually sustained. Feed your faith by filling it with God's Word, and then make sure you act on that Word. This is very important. The word of man is what man is; the Word of God is what God is. If you want to live like a child of God, then you have to believe His Word.

Faith means having total conviction concerning God's promises to man. Believing God is simply taking God at His Word, making requests based on His Word, and then acting as if you own the title deed to what He has promised. Remember that it is better, safer, healthier, and more reasonable to live by faith than to live by doubt or wishful thinking. People who live by doubt and wishful thinking get high blood pressure, frustration, tension, and anger. They are angry at the world because they can't see anything beyond their weak hope. However, those who live by faith defy the world's understanding. They have peace and joy even when they experience difficult situations. Like Jesus, they are able to sleep in the middle of a storm.

Faith is simply taking God at His Word.

God says, "You aren't supposed to live by what you see, but by what I told you." (See 2 Corinthians 5:7.) That means *what you know is more important than what you see.* Much of what you see contradicts what you know from God's Word. When you walk according to what you know, it will overcome what you see. It is what you see that is depressing you. You see that you have problems. However, if you know that God will deliver you from every tribulation (2 Tim. 4:18), then as far as you are concerned, you don't really have any problems; you are just experiencing a temporary discomfort.

I never use the word *problems* anymore. I haven't had "problems" for about thirty years. Why? It is because I understand that everything in the world is under God's command, including the devil. That is why the Bible says, *"We know that in all things God works for the good of those who love him, who have been called according to his purpose"* (Rom. 8:28). Everything works for my good, no matter what it is, because I'm called according to God's purpose and will. It is God's will that I live confidently in the knowledge that He calls *"things that are not as though they were"* (Rom. 4:17). If I live only by what I see, I am living in sin. *"Everything that does not come from faith is sin"* (Rom. 14:23). There are many such sinners in the church—people who are in rebellion against God's will because they are living only by what they see. Faith grows out of one thing—the Word of God.

God has promised certain things, and all His promises are already "yes." (See 2 Corinthians 1:18–20.) In other words, He wants to give you everything He promised. Some of the promises in the Bible were spoken to a specific person or group of people. Yet the Bible indicates that Jesus made His promises accessible to everybody. *"No matter how many promises God has made, they are 'Yes' in Christ"* (2 Cor. 1:20). Jesus made the contract, which God gave to a specific person or group, everyone's contract. However, you have to qualify in the same way they had to qualify—by using your faith. Once you know the promise, you don't have to say, "If it is God's will." A person prays in that way only when he isn't sure about something. God doesn't go against what He has promised. That is why praying the Word is so important.

Sometimes God will back you into a corner and take away all your other alternatives because He wants to show you His miracle-working power. Perhaps you are facing a difficult situation and have come to the place where you can say, "I've tried everything else. All I have now is what God has said to me." Whenever God reduces you to His Word, if that's all you have to go on, you're about to receive a miracle! As long as you have a scheme to fall back on, you aren't going to see the miracle. However, when you say, "I can't do anything else; I don't know what to do. If God doesn't come through, I'm going under," then God says, "I like this situation. I'm going to get involved in this, because I love to do the impossible!"

If you have faith in God's Word, God will take what is "impossible" and make it seem like an everyday thing. He enabled Sarah in the Old Testament and Elizabeth in the New Testament to bear sons when they were barren and past childbearing age. He enabled Mary to become the mother of Jesus when she was unmarried and a virgin. I like Mary's response to the angel who brought her this news: *"I am the Lord's servant....May it be to me as you have said"* (Luke 1:38). In other words, "Lord, do whatever You want to do."

Your "problem" circumstance excites God because He knows you now have to rely on faith, which will enable you to receive His promise. God's dreams are always in contrast to your difficulties. God knows what things look like to you. He gives you the promise ahead of the blessing so that when it comes, you'll know it came from Him.

Everything I have, I have received through prayer. When you pray God's Word in faith, things that have been bound up will suddenly open up. You will say, "But I had been trying to accomplish that for ten years!" Yes, but you hadn't prayed according to God's Word and trusted in God's faithfulness until now. Belief will open doors that hard work cannot unlock. God says if you believe Him, He is going to give you the best of the land, the fat of the land. (See Genesis 45:18.) For example, you are going to have the best position at your workplace. God will first put you in a lower position in order to check your attitude. He will keep you there for a while to develop your character. Once you qualify, God will say, "It's time to move up!" Even if people try to thwart you, prayer will foil their plans. Expect God to act, and look for the fulfillment of the promise—or it may pass you by.

Belief will open doors that hard work cannot unlock.

When the local church in Jerusalem met and prayed for Peter when he was imprisoned for preaching the Gospel, an angel delivered him from prison. Peter went to the house where many of the believers were praying and knocked on the door. When the believers saw that it was Peter, they were astonished, even though they had been praying for his release. (See Acts 12:1–16.) I believe they were astonished for several reasons: first, they didn't really believe in the power of prayer; second, they didn't believe God could deliver Peter under the difficult conditions he was facing; and third, they didn't believe God could answer prayer that quickly. Are you facing difficult circumstances? Are you expecting God to deliver you, or are you thinking along the same lines as those believers did? God is able to answer quickly—in any situation.

Let's look at what could be considered the ultimate passage on prayer. First John 5:13–15 pulls together everything we have been discussing. It begins, *"I write these things to you who believe in the name of the Son of God..."* (v. 13). Does this verse apply to you? If you believe in the name of the Son of God it does. The passage continues, *"...so that you may know that you have eternal life"* (v. 13). John was saying, "I'm writing these things so that you can know you are connected to God." Then he said, *"This is the confidence we have in approaching God..."* (v. 14). What is that confidence? *"...that if we ask anything according to his will, he hears us"* (v. 14).

Here's that conditional word *"if"* again: *"If we ask anything according to his will...."* God's Word is His will. His Word is His desire, His desire is His intent, and His intent is His purpose. *"If we ask anything according to his will, he hears us."* You can be sure God always hears your prayers—one hundred percent of the time—when you pray according to His will. Who does God hear when you pray His Word? He hears Himself. God will hear you when He hears the words He Himself has spoken.

Is there anything more important in prayer than for God to hear you? The passage tells us what happens when this takes place: *"And if we know that he hears us—whatever we ask—we know that **we have** what we asked of him"* (v. 15, emphasis added).

God's plan for your life is even bigger than your plans. However, to enter into that plan, you have to believe in it and affirm it by what you say. The reason Jesus' life was so successful was that He didn't speak His own words; He spoke God's words.

> *For I did not speak of my own accord, but the Father who sent me commanded me what to say and how to say it. I know that his command leads to eternal life. So whatever I say is just what the Father has told me to say.* (John 12:49–50)

> *The words I say to you are not just my own. Rather, it is the Father, living in me, who is doing his work....He who does not love me will not obey my teaching. These words you hear are not my own; they belong to the Father who sent me.* (John 14:10, 24)

Do we need anything clearer than this? This is the secret to living a victorious life of faith. It was a major key to Jesus' power on earth. Jesus Christ didn't invent words to say. He was always praying to God what God had said first. Why? Again, it is because God watches over His Word to fulfill it. Jesus' works were the Father's works because His words were the Father's words. His miracles were the Father's miracles because His words were the Father's words. He knew who He was, what He believed, and what to say, and that combination brought Him victory on earth.

Speaking the Father's words was the primary secret of Jesus' power.

The same can be true for us if we follow His example.

THE WORD SAYS MUCH ABOUT PRAYER

Another reason the Bible builds faith—and therefore gives power—is that it is the greatest Book ever written about how God answers the faith-filled prayers of His people. Hebrews 11:1 says that *"the ancients"* were commended for the fact that they did not live by what they could see, but by what God told them. They believed and acted upon it, and it worked.

The men and women of the Bible were not super-saints. They were people just like us. They received answers to prayer as they put their faith in God, trusting in His character and Word. The Bible makes this very clear:

Elijah was a man just like us. He prayed earnestly that it would not rain, and it did not rain on the land for three and a half years. Again he prayed, and the heavens gave rain, and the earth produced its crops.
(James 5:17–18)

The Scriptures say, *"God does not show favoritism"* (Acts 10:34). This means He will not treat us any differently than believers in ancient times, except that now we have an additional advantage—the atonement and prayers of Christ on our behalf, as well as the intercession of the Spirit. It is through the powerful examples of believers in the Bible that we are encouraged to have faith that God can and will intervene on our behalf. Here are just a few examples:

- A servant (Abraham's chief servant) and a king (Solomon) both asked for wisdom, and God gave it in each case. (See Genesis 24:1–27; 1 Kings 3:4–14.)
- Hannah asked God for blessing and deliverance from her distress, and God granted her request. (See 1 Samuel 1:1–20.)
- Moses and Daniel interceded for the nation of Israel, and God heard and answered in His mercy. (See Exodus 32:1–14; Daniel 9.)
- Nehemiah prayed for the restoration of Jerusalem (Nehemiah 1:1–11) and was granted favor and protection in his work to rebuild the walls. (See the book of Nehemiah.)
- Both Anna and Simeon, after lifetimes of faithful devotion to God, received signs that confirmed God's promise of a Redeemer. (See Luke 2:25–38.)
- Paul and Cornelius received knowledge concerning the way of salvation after they had prayed. (See Acts 9:1–20, especially verse 11; Acts 10.)
- Jesus at His baptism (Luke 3:21–22), and the disciples at Pentecost (Acts 1:14; 2:1–4), received the Holy Spirit after prayer.
- Peter and John received revelation and insight while they were praying. (See Acts 10:9–15; 11:1–18; Revelation 1:9–10.)
- Paul and Silas were delivered from prison after praying and singing to God. (See Acts 16:16–34.)

We know from reading about the lives of these believers that many of them struggled with doubts, were inclined to mistakes and failures, and had to learn by experience. However, we also see the faithfulness and love of God in teaching them His ways, coming to their aid, and strengthening them for the purposes He had in mind for them. The Bible is filled with stories of the power of God to save, heal, and bless. These accounts are God's faith messages to us, telling us that He will intervene on our behalf, also. We are His beloved children; we have been redeemed by His Son and are being prepared to rule and reign with Him in eternity. *"He who did not spare his own Son, but gave him up for us all—how will he not also, along with him, graciously give us all things?"* (Rom. 8:32).

THE WORD PREPARES THE PRAY-ER FOR PRAYER

Last, the Word gives power in prayer by enabling us to prepare for it and maintain communion with God. Psalm 119 tells us that when we wholeheartedly embrace the Word, it will keep our lives in line with God's will so that nothing will hinder us from walking in His ways and receiving answers to our prayers: *"Blessed are they who keep his statutes and seek him with all their heart. They do nothing wrong; they walk in his ways....I have hidden your word in my heart that I might not sin against you"* (vv. 2–3, 11).

As we learned earlier, Aaron had to prepare himself to enter God's presence before offering sacrifices on the Day of Atonement. We need to offer our lives every day as living sacrifices to God so we can have continual fellowship with Him. *"Offer your bodies as living sacrifices, holy and pleasing to God—this is your spiritual act of worship"* (Rom. 12:1). Then, as our minds are transformed by reading and meditating on the Word, we will know the will of God, and we will pray confidently and effectively:

> *Do not conform any longer to the pattern of this world, but be transformed by the renewing of your mind.* ***Then you will be able to test and approve what God's will is—his good, pleasing and perfect will.***
> (v. 2, emphasis added)

What a tremendous gift the Word of God is to us! It gives us the power to know and do the will of God, the power to pray with certainty and boldness in all situations, and the power to know that God hears us when we pray according to His will. *"And if we know that he hears us—whatever we ask—we know that we have what we asked of him"* (1 John 5:15).

LET'S PRAY TOGETHER

Heavenly Father,

You have said that those who hear the Word and receive it, those who allow it to sink into their hearts, are like good soil (Matt. 13:23). Yet the power is in the Word. It is the Word that will bring forth good fruit in us and spring up within us to everlasting life. We ask You to fulfill Your Word in our lives. Make us good soil that brings forth good fruit. Your Word has caused us to believe that you will answer prayer offered in faith and according to Your will. We set ourselves in agreement with You that everything we pray will be answered "yes." We will both expect and prepare for the answer. Give us the confidence that if You said it, You will do it; if You promised it, it will come to pass. Thank You for Your Word. Thank You for the faith that You have given us. Help us to expect a miracle. We pray this in the name of Jesus, our High Priest, who sits at Your right hand and intercedes for us. Amen.

PUTTING PRAYER INTO PRACTICE

Ask yourself:

- A cardinal principle of answered prayer is that I believe in the trustworthiness of the One to whom I am praying. Do I believe that God is honorable and that He will keep His Word?

- Do I think of the Word as being alive and active on my behalf, or is reading the Bible just a religious obligation to me?

- When I read in the Bible about God answering the prayers of His people, do I allow it to build my faith for my own circumstances, or do I think I am just reading some interesting stories?

Action Steps:

- Focus this week on abiding in Christ and having His words abide in you (John 15:7), so that the Word can be inside you to work powerfully in your life. Spend time worshipping and fellowshipping with God, reading and mediating on His Word, praying and fasting.

- Meditate on verses that speak to the various needs in your life in order to build your faith in God and His Word. (For example: *wisdom*—James 1:5; *salvation*—John 3:16; *healing*—1 Peter 2:24; *finances*—Philippians 4:19; *prosperity*—Isaiah 1:19–20; *provision*—Matthew 7:11.)

- Examine the lives of three people in the Bible who offered effectual prayers to God. What were their prayers like? What were their lives like? What had God promised them? What did God show or do for them in answering their prayers? Write down your findings and refer to them when you are in similar situations.

Principles

1. Whatever we ask God to do in our lives, in the lives of others, or in the world, must be based on His Word. God's purpose is to be both the motivation and the content for our prayers.

2. Without God's Word as their basis, our prayers have no foundation. They are based merely on our opinions, desires, and feelings. Such prayers are powerless to effect change.

3. Prayer is speaking the Word to God exactly as He gave it to us.

4. There is no difference between what the people in the Bible were given by God as the basis for their effective prayers and what you and I are given to work with. Both rely on what God has given all mankind—His Word.

5. God wants to use His power in the world; however, for Him to do so, we must know how to appropriate His Word. We must understand what it is and how to apply it.

6. God Himself is speaking in the Word.

7. God's Word is the foundation of His power. His power is a reflection of His greatness.

8. The Word reveals God's nature to us.

9. A cardinal principle of answered prayer is belief in the trustworthiness of the One to whom you're praying. *Belief is trust in action.*

10. The Word is alive and active on our behalf.

11. The Word builds faith in us.

12. The Word says much about how God answers the prayers of believers.

13. The Word prepares the pray-er for prayer.

Chapter Eleven

The Power of Jesus' Name

We must be able to legally use the authority behind the power of Jesus' name in order to obtain results in prayer.

One of the most important elements of effective prayer is using the name of Jesus. In conjunction with praying according to the Word, praying in the name of Jesus gives our prayers tremendous power.

MAGIC FORMULA?

Many believers' prayers aren't being answered because they misunderstand what it means to pray in the name of Jesus. We tend to think we can pray any type of prayer and then say, "In the name of Jesus, amen," believing that the phrase alone is what makes our prayers effective with God. It doesn't work that way.

We shouldn't try to dignify or sanctify our prayers by tacking the name of Jesus on at the end. As we learned earlier in this book, Jesus' name is not a magic formula or password that guarantees automatic acceptance of all our prayers. When the Bible says we are to pray in the name of Jesus, it's not referring to the word *J-e-s-u-s* as such, because that's just the English word for the name of the Son of God; other languages translate His name using different words. It's not the word but what the name represents that makes the difference. If you name your son Bill Gates, that doesn't mean he owns billions of dollars. If you call yourself Sarah Hughes, that doesn't mean you have an Olympic gold medal in ice-skating. The words themselves don't mean anything unless there is substance and reality behind them. Likewise, we're not effective in prayer just by using the word *Jesus,* but in understanding the significance of who He really is and appropriating His power through faith in His name.

We see a clear demonstration of this truth in the account of the sons of Sceva in the book of Acts.

> *Some Jews who went around driving out evil spirits tried to invoke the name of the Lord Jesus over those who were demon-possessed. They would say, "In the name of Jesus, whom Paul preaches, I command you to come out." Seven sons of Sceva, a Jewish chief priest, were doing this. One day the evil spirit answered them, "Jesus I know, and I know about Paul, but who are you?" Then the man who had the evil spirit jumped on them and overpowered them all. He gave them such a beating that they ran out of the house naked and bleeding. When this became known to the Jews and Greeks living in Ephesus, they were all seized with fear, and the name of the Lord Jesus was held in high honor.* (Acts 19:13–17)

This story reveals that someone can use the name *Jesus* all he wants, but he will still have no authority over the devil if (1) he isn't in proper relationship with Christ, and (2) he doesn't understand how to use Jesus' name. *We must be able to legally use the authority behind the power of Jesus' name in order to obtain results in prayer.*

Think about it: What does the law say about someone who uses a name without legal authority? The law calls it fraud. Suppose you went to my bank and said you wanted to withdraw money from my account. The teller would ask to see your identification. In other words, he wouldn't necessarily take your word for it, but would require something deeper—proof of identification. If you were to say, "Oh, I left my ID at home," he would answer, "Well, then you can just leave that money in the bank." Or suppose you stole a check that was written to me, forged my signature on the back, and tried to cash it. The teller would check your handwriting with a sample of my signature on file. When he saw that it was different, he would call security and say, "Hold this one for the police."

Most of us wouldn't think of trying to commit fraud on a bank, but we do a similar thing all the time in prayer. We pray hard, saying, "In the name of Jesus." The Father says, "Show me some ID. Are you in right relationship with My Son? Are you praying based on the righteousness of Christ or on your own merits? Do you understand who my Son is and do you believe in His authority and power?" As the sons of Sceva found out, it doesn't work to pray in Jesus' name without knowing who He is and praying in faith according to that knowledge.

OUR COVENANTAL RIGHTS

God does not owe us anything. We have no claim on Him outside Christ's work of grace on our behalf. Christ redeemed us from our sins, or trespasses (Eph. 1:7). When you trespass, you are doing something illegal. Similarly, someone who doesn't know God or is not in proper relationship with God through Christ cannot legally do business with God. Yet because of Jesus, we can be forgiven of our trespasses. He cancelled our sins through His sacrifice on the cross and delivered us from the power of sin, so now we can have legal access to God through His name. No one can claim power through Jesus' name without having official-child-of-God status. *"But as many as received him, to them gave he power to become the sons of God, even to them that believe on his name"* (John 1:12 KJV). And remember that, since Jesus won back mankind's dominion over the earth, we can also legally rule on the earth again through His authority.

The authority we have in Jesus' name is a covenantal authority.

The authority we have in His name through prayer is a covenantal authority; it is based on our covenant relationship with God through Christ. *"But the ministry Jesus has received is as superior to theirs* [the priests of Israel] *as the covenant of which he is mediator is superior to the old one, and it is founded on better promises"* (Heb. 8:6). We can pray to God directly in Jesus' name because He has given us authority to do so based on the new covenant. Seven times in the New Testament Jesus made a statement such as the following, giving us the legal right to use His name with God.

> *In that day you will no longer ask me anything. I tell you the truth, my Father will give you whatever you ask in my name. Until now you have not asked for anything in my name. Ask and you will receive, and your joy will be complete. Though I have been speaking figuratively, a time is coming when I will no longer use this kind of language but will tell you plainly about my Father. In that day you will ask in my name. I am not saying that I will ask the Father on your behalf. No, the Father himself loves you because you have loved me and have believed that I came from God.* (John 16:23–27)

Therefore, the strength of prayers prayed in the name of Jesus is covenantal authority. We pray to the Father based on our relationship with Christ, who is Lord over the new covenant. Philippians 2:10 says, *"At the name of Jesus every knee should bow, in heaven and on earth and under the earth."* Because Christ restored us to our relationship and rights with both God and the earth, His name is our legal authority—whether we are dealing with *"heaven"* (with God), *"earth"* (with men), or *"under the earth"* (with Satan).

In essence, Jesus' name is our legal authority to transact spiritual business with God. *"For there is one God and one mediator between God and men, the man Christ Jesus, who gave himself as a ransom for all men—the testimony given in its proper time"* (1 Tim. 2:5–6).

WHAT'S IN A NAME?

Once we see that we have authority through the name of Jesus, we need to understand the substance behind His name. This requires an awareness of the Bible's emphasis on the meaning of names. Today, most people choose names for their children based on how the names sound or look. However, in the Scriptures, the name of someone (or something) usually symbolized the essence of his nature. It represented the person's collective attributes and characteristics—his nature, power, and glory.

First Corinthians 15:41 says, *"There is one glory of the sun, another glory of the moon, and another glory of the stars; for one star differs from another star in glory"* (NKJV). The glory of something is its best expression of itself. You can see a flower in its true glory when it is in full bloom. You can see a leopard or a lion in its true glory when it is at its prime strength. You can see the sun in its true glory at twelve noon. The glory of a thing is when it is at its full, true self. Again, when the Bible refers to someone's name, it is generally talking about that person's true nature, or glory.

In the Bible, a person's name symbolized the essence of his nature.

For example, God gave Adam the privilege of naming Eve—of encapsulating Eve's attributes. Adam actually named Eve twice—first as a description of her origin and the second time as a description of who she would become in fulfillment of her purpose. First, he said, *"This is now bone of my bones and flesh of my flesh; she shall be called 'woman,' for she was taken out of man"* (Gen. 2:23). Later, the Bible says, *"Adam named his wife Eve, because she would become the mother of all the living"* (Gen. 3:20). The Hebrew word for Eve is *chavvah*, meaning "life-giver." Her name describes the essence of her nature as the mother of mankind.

Let's look at a few more examples of biblical figures and the significance of their names. At times, God would *change* the names of His people to reflect the promises He had made to them and the purposes He had for them, which went far beyond their own or their parents' expectations.

- In Genesis 17:4–5, Abram's name, which meant "exalted father" or "high father," was changed to Abraham, meaning "father of a multitude," reflecting the promise that *"Abraham will surely become a great and powerful nation, and all nations on earth will be blessed through him"* (Gen. 18:18).

- In Genesis 32:27–28, Jacob's name, which meant "supplanter," was changed to Israel, meaning "he will rule as

God" or "a prince of God." This reflected the fact that the great nation of Israel would come from his line—the nation that was meant to be God's earthly representative by being *a kingdom of priests and a holy nation"* (Exod. 19:6).

* In John 1:42, Jesus changed Simon's name, which is derived from a Hebrew word meaning "hearing," to Cephas, meaning "a rock" or "a stone." The English translation of this word is "Peter." Peter's new name signified his role in establishing and leading the church in its infancy. (See Matthew 16:18.)

Why does God put such emphasis on people's names? It is because mankind is made in His image, and He places great significance on His own name. Using our earlier definition, God's name symbolizes the essence of His nature. It represents His collective attributes and characteristics—His nature, power, and glory. Remember that, since there is total consistency between who God is and what He says and does, He has complete integrity, or wholeness—the definition of *holiness.* The main reason we are commanded not to use the name of God in vain (Exod. 20:7) is that His name does not just represent who He is, but also, it *is* who He is.

God revealed this tremendous truth to Moses:

> *Moses said to God, "Suppose I go to the Israelites and say to them, 'The God of your fathers has sent me to you,' and they ask me, 'What is his name?' Then what shall I tell them?" God said to Moses, "I AM WHO I AM. This is what you are to say to the Israelites: 'I AM has sent me to you.'" God also said to Moses, "Say to the Israelites, 'The LORD, the God of your fathers—the God of Abraham, the God of Isaac and the God of Jacob—has sent me to you.' This is my name forever, the name by which I am to be remembered from generation to generation."* (Exod. 3:13–15)

In other words, God was saying, "I *am* My name. Whatever I am, that's what I'm called." When you translate this concept into English, it goes something like this: "My name is whatever I am at the time I am it." This is because God is our all-sufficiency, and His name differs depending on what our need is at a particular time. In effect, God is saying to us, "If you need bread, then pray, 'Father, You are my Bread.' When you acknowledge that I am your Provider and Sustenance, then I become Bread to you. If you are thirsty, then pray, "Father, You are my Water.' I manifest the characteristic of whatever you need." Moreover, by calling Himself *"the God of Abraham, the God of Isaac and the God of Jacob"* (Exod. 3:15), He affirms that He is a personal God who meets individual human needs. He is the God of real people—Abraham, Isaac, and Jacob. In the same way, He desires to be your God and to meet your individual needs, no matter what they are.

This is the reason there are so many names attributed to God in the Old Testament. To give you a few additional examples, He is variously described as *"a consuming fire"* (Deut. 4:24), *"the shadow of a great rock in a weary land"* (Isa. 32:2 NKJV), and *"shepherd"* (Ps. 23:1)—three distinct attributes that reflect specific aspects of God's nature and character. Yet God's overarching name, I AM, encompasses all His nature and attributes.

THE NAME OF JESUS

Let's look now at how the Bible's emphasis on the meaning of names—especially God's name—applies to praying in the name of Jesus. Since a person's name represents his collective attributes and characteristics, the names of the second person of the Trinity refer to all that He is, both as the Son of God and as the Son of Man—all of His nature, power, and glory.

Like God the Father, the Son has a variety of names that describe who He is. For example, in the Old Testament, some of His names are the *"Seed"* (Gen. 3:15 NKJV), *"the Branch"* (Zech. 6:12), and *"Immanuel* ["God with us"]*"* (Isa. 7:14). In the New Testament, the Son has many designations, but the first we read of is the name *Jesus*.

Neither of Jesus' earthly parents named Him because His name had already been given by God, His heavenly

Father. The angel Gabriel told Mary, *"You will be with child and give birth to a son, and you are to give him the name Jesus"* (Luke 1:31). Likewise, an angel of the Lord told Joseph, *"[Mary] will give birth to a son, and you are to give him the name Jesus, because he will save his people from their sins"* (Matt. 1:21).

Why did God name Jesus? First, to show that Jesus was His Son. Second, because Jesus' name had to reflect who He is. The name *Jesus* means "Savior." He was called Savior because that is what He came to earth as a human being to accomplish—the salvation of the world. *"He will save his people from their sins."* Therefore, *Jesus* is the name of Christ in His humanity—as the Son of Man. However, *I AM* is the name of Christ in His divinity—as the Son of God.

Jesus Christ is the revelation of God in human form.

"'I tell you the truth,' Jesus answered, 'before Abraham was born, I am!'" (John 8:58). Jesus Christ is the revelation of God in human form. Because He is fully divine as well as fully human, He is ascribed a variety of names, just as God is.

On one occasion, Jesus said, *"I am the bread of life"* (John 6:35). Not long afterward, He indicated that He is also the water of life: *"If anyone is thirsty, let him come to me and drink"* (John 7:37). Like God the Father, the attributes that Jesus manifests reveal His glory and correspond to His people's needs. He referred to Himself as *"the way and the truth and the life"* (John 14:6) because He enables us to have access to the Father and receive spiritual life. He called Himself *"the true vine"* (John 15:1) because only by remaining in Him can we bear spiritual fruit.

Here is the key: If we want God to meet our need when we pray "in the name of Jesus," we must pray based on the divine name that meets our particular need at the time. This is how our prayers are answered. We don't receive answers to prayer by merely speaking Jesus' name, but by calling on His nature and attributes, which can meet our every need.

Let's look at a specific example of this in the Bible. What prompted Jesus to say, *"I am the resurrection and the life"* (John 11:25)? It was because He was confronted with a dead man named Lazarus. His name addressed the need at hand.

Lazarus had become sick and died. His sisters, Martha and Mary, knew Jesus as their honored friend. They greatly respected Jesus and called Him "Lord." They believed He was sent by God, but they did not fully understand who He was. He had stayed at the family's home many times and shared meals with them, but they hadn't realized they were entertaining *"the resurrection"* under their roof. Therefore, when Jesus told Martha, *"Your brother will rise again"* (v. 23), He wanted her to gain deeper insight into who He is.

Do you know Jesus only as Savior? Then that is probably all He will be to you. Do you know Him only as Healer? Then that is all He will be to you. Martha was limited in her knowledge of Jesus, so she answered Him, in effect, "Someday in the *future* when God raises the dead, my brother will be raised." (See John 11:23–24.) Jesus replied, *"**I am** the resurrection and the life. He who believes in me will live, even though he dies; and whoever lives and believes in me will never die. Do you believe this?"* (vv. 25–26, emphasis added). He was prompting Martha to call Him by the name that was needed, *"Resurrection."* In essence, He was saying to her, "Tell Me who you need Me to be. Call me that." What did she say? *"'Yes, Lord,' she told him, 'I believe that you are the Christ, the Son of God, who was to come into the world'"* (v. 27). Her word of faith in Christ helped to bring His resurrection power into the family's situation, and Lazarus was raised from the dead.

Have you ever heard anyone say, "If you need anything, just call me"? You can depend on Jesus like that when you're living the way you're supposed to live. The Bible says, *"The righteous will live by faith"* (Rom. 1:17). Have faith in Jesus and the many attributes His names represent.

If you believe in Jesus as your Savior and Redeemer from sin, that is wonderful because that is where everyone must start. However, He wants to reveal Himself to you in a deeper way. For example, do you know Him as the Savior of others, as well as yourself? If you want someone among your family and friends to be saved, then you can pray the name *Savior*. That's all you need to pray for the person who needs salvation: "Jesus, Savior, save Judy." Pray on behalf of others using the name that designates Jesus as the One who can save them. The Scripture says, *"Everyone who calls on the name of the Lord will be saved"* (Acts 2:21). Stand in their stead and call on the name of the Lord on their behalf.

The name of Jesus is given to you to use in relation to your needs.

Living by faith sometimes means saying what seems to us like the strangest things. For example, the Bible says, *"Let the weak say, 'I am strong'"* (Joel 3:10 NKJV). We're weak, but God tells us to say the opposite. He says, "Call on My strength. Call Me Jehovah Omnipotent." He isn't telling us to just use His name; He's calling on us to understand His nature and appropriate it in faith. It is not God's nature to be weak. If you are experiencing weakness, then you must call on the Lord your Strength (Ps. 18:1). If you are experiencing poverty, you must call on Jehovah-Jireh, your Provider. (See Genesis 22:8.) If your body is sick, you need to call on Jehovah-Rapha, the God who heals (Exod. 15:26). God is telling us not to dwell on the problem, but on His attribute that addresses the problem. Since He is the I AM, His attributes are as numerous as your needs—and beyond! For example, in the realm of your finances, do you know Him as Rent-Payer, Debt-Canceler, and Tuition-Provider? That is how we are to pray in the name of Jesus. It's important to understand that the name of Jesus is given to us to use in relation to our needs.

In John 11:11, when Jesus told His disciples, *"Lazarus has fallen asleep,"* was He contradicting the truth that Lazarus had died? Was He lying, or was He living at a higher level of life, knowing that He would be the Resurrection? At times we will confront situations that look final, but God will resurrect them. When it looks as if your business is dead, when the bank is about to foreclose and repossess everything, God says, in effect, "Don't say it's dead. Just say that it's sleeping." If it's sleeping, then sooner or later, it will wake up. If your marriage is in trouble, if your spouse has left, if you are saying, "It's over," God is saying, "It's not over; it's asleep." We lose many things in life because we declare them dead prematurely.

POWER OF ATTORNEY

Everything we have discussed about the name of Jesus and the covenant authority that we have through Him refers to Jesus' "power of attorney." Legally, when you give power of attorney to someone, it means that you appoint that person to represent you. You give the person the legal right and authority to speak for you and to do business in your name. Praying in the name of Jesus is giving Him power of attorney to intercede on your behalf when you make requests of the Father.

Jesus said,

I tell you the truth, my Father will give you whatever you ask in my name. Until now you have not asked for anything in my name. Ask and you will receive, and your joy will be complete. (John 16:23–24)

When Christ Jesus was on earth with the disciples, they didn't need to pray to the Father. When they needed food, Jesus provided it. When Peter's mother-in-law was sick, Jesus healed her. When they needed to pay taxes, Jesus supplied the money. When they needed a place to meet, Jesus had already made preparations for it. When they were with Jesus, they had everything they needed. If they wanted something, they asked Him for it directly. However, because Jesus was going to the Father, they would no longer be able to ask Him for anything directly. They would need to pray to the Father, and Jesus instructed them to do so in His name. Why? It is because the Father works through Christ.

Jesus is working on our behalf at the right hand of the Father.

Jesus is actively working on our behalf from His position at the right hand of the Father (Rom. 8:34). He is representing our interests to God: *"Therefore he is able to save completely those who come to God through him, because he always lives to intercede for them"* (Heb. 7:25). He is bringing glory to the Father by fulfilling the prayers we pray according to the Word:

> *I tell you the truth, anyone who has faith in me will do what I have been doing. He will do even greater things than these, because I am going to the Father. And I will do whatever you ask in my name, so that the Son may bring glory to the Father. You may ask me for anything in my name, and I will do it.*
> (John 14:12–14)

In other words, Jesus will see to it that we receive what we request. He will make sure that what is asked for is represented properly, so we will obtain the answer.

After Jesus spoke to His disciples about praying in His name, He immediately began to talk about the Holy Spirit, because the Spirit continues Jesus' ministry on earth. *"If you love me, you will obey what I command. And I will ask the Father, and he will give you another Counselor ["Comforter" KJV] to be with you forever—the Spirit of truth"* (vv. 15–17).

Jesus was saying, in effect, "I am going to the Father, but I will send you the Holy Spirit. He will be your Counselor. He will assist in exercising power of attorney by enabling you to pray. He will help you present your cases to God. He will help you get your situation clearly sorted out so you can present it to the Father in My name."

All through the New Testament we find reference to the work of the Holy Spirit. One of the repeated themes is that the Holy Spirit helps us in our weaknesses, especially when we do not know how to pray:

> *We do not know what we ought to pray for, but the Spirit himself intercedes for us with groans that words cannot express. And he who searches our hearts knows the mind of the Spirit, because the Spirit intercedes for the saints in accordance with God's will.* (Rom. 8:26–27)

The Power of Jesus' Name

Ephesians 6:18 instructs us to *"pray in the Spirit on all occasions with all kinds of prayers and requests,"* and Jude 20 says, *"Dear friends, build yourselves up in your most holy faith and pray in the Holy Spirit."*

Sometimes the Holy Spirit tells us what *not* to pray for. He will not give us clearance to pray for certain things. When this happens, we often will not feel at peace about praying for them. If the Holy Spirit is counseling you along those lines, don't ask for what you were going to ask. If you still go ahead and ask, you will be wasting your breath. We cannot present something to the Father if the timing is not right, or if it is out of God's will for our lives altogether. We cannot ask in Jesus' name if we know we are not praying according to God's purposes.

Jesus' Name Is the Key to Heaven

One of the things Jesus emphasized is that *"the Father loves the Son"* (John 3:35; John 5:20). This is a crucial truth in relation to prayer because, if the Father loves the Son, then the Father will do anything the Son wants. If the Father loves the Son and does whatever the Son asks, and if the Son is representing you, then you don't have to worry about your case being heard. That is why it is essential that you call upon Jesus' power of attorney when you pray.

If you want to do business with the Father, don't try to come without the name of Jesus, because *His name is the key to heaven.* Jesus didn't say to bring a list of saints to the Father when you pray. He didn't say to list some good people's names to help your case. Why would anyone want their help when we have the Son? Martha, Mary, Luke, Bartholomew, John, James, and the others were all faithful believers. Yet when Peter

No one but Jesus can be our legal channel to the Father.

encountered the man at the gate Beautiful, he healed him in the name of Jesus, not in the name of the believers. He said, in effect, "I don't have any silver and gold. All I have is a name, *the* name, and I'm about to do business with heaven. The Father is working, and I see you healed already.

Therefore, I am going to bring to earth what I see in heaven; but I have to do it through the legal channel." (See Acts 3:1–8.) No one but Jesus can be our legal channel to the Father.

We can appreciate the religious leaders in the world today and in history. However, Jesus said if we want to do business with the Father, we must come in His name alone. The Bible says, *"There is no other name under heaven given to men by which we must be saved"* (Acts 4:13). Our laws say that the person whose name is on the document as power of attorney is the only person who can legally give representation. According to God's Word, Jesus is the only one who can speak for you: *"For there is one God and one mediator between God and men, the man Christ Jesus"* (1 Tim. 2:5). The Scripture also says,

> *Therefore God exalted* [Jesus] *to the highest place and gave him the name that is above every name, that at the name of Jesus every knee should bow, in heaven and on earth and under the earth.*
> (Phil. 2:9–10)

If you want the knee of poverty to bow, you have to use the right name. If you want the knee of sickness to bow, don't use anyone else's name. If you want the knee of depression to bow, use Jesus' name.

Sometimes people will give testimonies about how they were almost robbed or how someone was going to break into their homes, but they just said, "Jesus!" and the robbers ran away. Those robbers ran because the power of the Savior was present. We need to use the name.

Jesus' name is power in heaven, and every tongue will eventually confess that Jesus is Lord—Lord of everything. This truth is the basis on which we are to fulfill the Great Commission—telling others about the power of Jesus' name to save and deliver.

> *Then Jesus came to* [His followers] *and said, "All authority in heaven and on earth has been given to me. Therefore go and make disciples of all nations, baptizing them in the name of the Father and of the Son and of the Holy Spirit."* (Matt. 28:18–19)

Because he acted on Christ's authority, the apostle Paul, in addition to the other apostles, *"preached fearlessly in the name of Jesus"* (Acts 9:27). The courage and boldness we need to make disciples of all nations comes from the authority we have been given in Jesus.

CALL ON THE NAME OF THE LORD

The Bible says, *"The name of the LORD is a strong tower; the righteous run to it and are safe"* (Prov. 18:10). Perhaps you have been praying for something for a long time. If you need healing, use the name of Jesus as you never have before and apply His name to your situation. Perhaps you need deliverance from bad habits. To break those chains, you must use the power of His name.

Whatever you need, call on Him to fulfill that need based on who He is. Use what He has given you: His nature; His attributes; the authority to pray in His name so you can ask the Father to manifest His power in your life and in the lives of others. *Call on the name of the Lord.*

LET'S PRAY TOGETHER

Heavenly Father,
"How majestic is your name in all the earth!" (Ps. 8:1, 9). Your Word says that at the name of Jesus, every knee will bow and every tongue confess that Jesus is Lord over everything (Phil. 2:9–10). Jesus said if we ask for anything in His name, You will do it (John 16:23). We know that we cannot ask in Jesus' name unless we ask what is according to Your will. However, we also know that when we ask in your Son's name, He will present our requests to You properly. He will pray in accordance with Your will. He will pray for us when we don't know what to say. He will appeal our case. So, Lord, we ask that Your will be done. There is no other name by which we make our requests but the name of Jesus. We call on the power of His name to meet all our needs. We pray in the name of Jesus, whose name is above all names. Amen!

PUTTING PRAYER INTO PRACTICE

Ask yourself:

- Have I prayed in the name of Jesus without thinking about what that name really means?
- When I pray in Jesus' name, do I think about whether my own life is a representation of His character and life?
- What specific attributes of Jesus meet my particular needs today?

Action Steps:

- Jesus' name is the only name that can activate power in heaven. Apply what you have learned in this chapter by thinking about your needs and the needs of others, and calling on His name as your power of attorney. Since He is the I AM, His attributes are as numerous as your needs. He is Savior, Healer, Strengthener, Freedom, Joy, Wisdom, Kindness, Friendship, Vision-Giver, Sustainer, Rent Payer, Business Grower, and so much more.
- Take time this week to worship the Lord for all His marvelous attributes. Ask Him to forgive you for taking His name lightly or misusing His name, and then purpose in your heart always to honor His name.
- *"The name of the LORD is a strong tower; the righteous run to it and are safe"* (Prov. 18:10). Whenever you are in a difficult situation, instead of becoming fearful, anxious, or angry, run to the name of the Lord in prayer and call on Him as your Salvation and Righteousness and as your Protector and Defender.

Principles

1. Jesus' name is not a magic formula that guarantees automatic acceptance of all our prayers.

2. We must be able to legally use the authority behind the power of Jesus' name in order to obtain results in prayer.

3. The authority we have in Jesus' name through prayer is a covenantal authority because it is based on our covenant relationship with God through Christ.

4. In the Scriptures, the name of someone (or something) symbolized the essence of his nature. It represented the person's collective attributes and characteristics—his nature, power, and glory.

5. God's overarching name, I AM, encompasses all His nature and attributes.

6. The names of the second person of the Trinity refer to all that He is, both as the Son of God and as the Son of Man—all of His nature, power, and glory.

7. *Jesus* is the name of Christ in His humanity—as the Son of Man. *I AM* is the name of Christ in His divinity—as the Son of God. *"'I tell you the truth,' Jesus answered, 'before Abraham was born, I am!'"* (John 8:58).

8. If we want God to meet our need when we pray "in the name of Jesus," we must pray based on the divine name that meets our particular need at that time.

9. To pray in the name of Jesus is to give Him power of attorney on our behalf when we make requests of the Father.

10. The Holy Spirit continues Jesus' ministry on earth. He assists in exercising power of attorney by enabling us to pray when we don't know how to pray.

11. Jesus' name is the *only* name that can activate power in heaven.

12. The authority of Jesus' name is the basis on which we are to fulfill the Great Commission.

Chapter Twelve

Understanding Fasting

A fast is a conscious, intentional decision to abstain for a time from the pleasure of eating in order to gain vital spiritual benefits.

All the greatest saints in the Bible fasted. Moses, David, Nehemiah, Jeremiah, Daniel, Anna, Paul, Peter, and even Jesus Himself fasted.

Have you ever said to yourself anything like the following? "I wish I had the faith of Joshua, who made the sun stand still." "I wish I could be like Peter, whose shadow falling on people resulted in their healing—or Paul, whose very clothes caused the people who touched them to be healed or delivered." "I'd like to be like John, who received the Revelation from God." We admire these believers, but we don't realize why such spiritual power was manifested in their lives. It was because they committed themselves to high standards in the practice of their faith so that God could use them to fulfill His purposes. In accordance with this, prayer and fasting were a normal part of their lives.

Fasting is one of the pillars of the Christian faith. It is mentioned in Scripture one-third as much as prayer. Yet most believers put fasting in the background of their experience as believers. Many consider the regular practice of fasting to be almost fanatical.

This was not the case in the past. Fasting used to be seen as valuable and significant in the Christian church. Now it has become a lost art. So little is taught and practiced in regard to fasting that it is not understood by most believers, especially young Christians who are just coming into the body of Christ. They don't hear about or see any older believers fasting, so they conclude that it is something that has only historic significance.

When I bring up the topic of fasting with believers today, they inevitably have many questions:

- Should every believer fast?
- Is there any virtue in fasting?
- How does fasting add to our prayer lives?
- Does fasting mean simply to abstain from food?
- When are we to fast?
- Can a person fast, but not pray?
- What is the spiritual significance of fasting?

Fasting has been part of my lifestyle for the past thirty-four years of my walk with the Lord. I started fasting at age fourteen and have developed a tremendous love for this wonderful experience. In this chapter, I want to give you some general guidelines to help you understand what fasting is and why God says we are to fast.

FASTING IS A NATURAL PART OF THE CHRISTIAN LIFE

First, fasting should be a natural part of the life of a believer. In the same way that we practice the habits of reading the Bible and prayer, we should also practice the habit of fasting.

Prayer and fasting are equal parts of a single ministry. In Matthew 6:5–6, Jesus said, *"**When** you pray..."* (emphasis added). He didn't say, "If you pray," but *"When you pray."* In the same passage, He said, *"**When** you fast...."* (vv. 16–17, emphasis added). Just as prayer is not an option for the believer, fasting is not an option. It is a natural expectation of God for His people. Christ is saying to us, "If you love Me, you will pray and fast." There are times when the Holy Spirit will move upon a person or group of people and supernaturally give them a desire to fast. Yet the majority of the time, fasting is an act of our faith and our wills. It is a decision we make based on our obedience to Christ. Even if we want to eat, we temporarily choose not to because of our love for Him.

Understanding Fasting

THE PURPOSE OF FASTING

Fasting is *intentional* abstinence from eating. Sometimes people confuse hunger with fasting. They will say, "Well, I was so busy that I didn't eat today. I'll make that a fast." That wasn't a fast, because you had planned to eat but just didn't have the time. In the Old Testament, the Hebrew word for fast is *tsum*. It means "to cover over the mouth." In the New Testament, the Greek word is *nesteuo*. It means "to abstain from food." A fast is a conscious, intentional decision to abstain for a time from the pleasure of eating in order to gain vital spiritual benefits. True fasting involves the following:

Seeking God

First, fasting is a time set apart to seek the face of God. It means abstaining from other things that you find pleasure in for the purpose of giving your whole heart to God in prayer. When you fast, you're telling God, "My prayer and the answers I'm seeking are more important than my pleasure in eating."

Putting God First

Second, fasting means putting God first, focusing all your attention on Him alone—not on His gifts or blessings, but on God Himself. It shows God how much you love and appreciate Him. In this way, fasting is a point of intimacy with God. God will reveal Himself only to people who want to **Fasting is putting God first in your life.** know Him. He says, *"You will seek me and find me when you seek me with all your heart"* (Jer. 29:13).

When you fast, it means that you want to be with God more than you want to spend time with other people, that you want Him more than your business or your busy-ness. Your fasting shows God that He is first in your life. It is a purposeful commitment to Him. If you tell God, "Oh, Lord, I want to see Your face," while your mind is wandering, God will say, "I cannot show you My face when you're not looking at Me."

Fasting means God alone is who you want. You don't want what He has to give you; you want Him. It's not a matter of you trying to get something from God. It's a matter of you trying to get *to* God. That's because, when you find God Himself, you will discover that everything you need comes with Him.

Creating an Environment for Prayer

Third, fasting is a time to foster a sensitive environment for the working of prayer. Whenever you read about fasting in the Bible, it always has the word *prayer* coupled with it. In the Old Testament, people fasted in conjunction with wholehearted prayer in times of mourning and repentance. It was also used as a point of deliverance from various situations. Often, when an enemy was challenging the people of God, the Israelites would commit themselves to several days of fasting. They would say, in effect, "We will fast until the Lord tells us what to do." The Lord would respond and give them a strategy, and they would win the battle.

Therefore, fasting adds to our prayers the environment for God to work. It enables us to see the fulfillment of God's Word and purposes for us as individuals and as the body of Christ.

Interceding for Others

Fourth, fasting is a form of intercession for others. In the majority of the cases in the Bible, when any person or people fasted, it was on behalf of the needs of others, whether it was a national problem or a family situation. They fasted to bring God into their circumstances. I believe those who fast also benefit from their obedience in fasting. However, the main purpose for fasting is to benefit others. Fasting goes beyond just praying, because sometimes our prayers can be very selfish. We often pray only for our own wants and needs. Fasting takes prayer into a completely different realm.

For example, when Jesus was about to begin His ministry, the price He had to pay was forty days and nights of fasting (Luke 4:1–2). He needed to consecrate Himself for the difficult task of fulfilling God's purpose of redeeming the world. Also, just before Jesus chose His twelve disciples, He spent the night in prayer (Luke 6:12–16). Right before His crucifixion, He prayed on behalf of those whom God had given Him and for those who would believe in Him through the disciples' testimony (John 17:6–26). What was Jesus' motivation for fasting and praying? It was for the sake of His disciples and for believers down through the ages who would place their faith in Him.

> [The scribes and Pharisees] *said to* [Jesus], *"John's disciples often fast and pray, and so do the disciples of the Pharisees, but yours go on eating and drinking." Jesus answered, "Can you make the guests of the bridegroom fast while he is with them? But the time will come when the bridegroom will be taken from them; in those days they will fast."* (Luke 5:33–35)

Christ was saying, "As long as I'm with the disciples, they aren't going to fast, because I fast for them. But the day will come when I will go to be with the Father; then they will fast." Why were the disciples going to fast if Jesus had fasted for them? They were going to fast for the world, so the world could receive the power of God through their faith and testimony. Likewise, when we fast, we are to fast for other people's benefit.

THE RESULTS OF FASTING

We need to understand the value and significance of emptying ourselves of food and filling ourselves with God. Fasting enables us to increase our spiritual capacity. It exerts discipline over our physical appetites. It brings the body under subjection to what the spirit desires. We are spirits, but we live in bodies. Most of the time our bodies control us. When you fast, your spirit increases its control over your body. Fasting enables you to discipline your body so that the body becomes a servant of the Lord, rather than the master of your spirit. Your body begins to obey your spirit rather than its own impulses and habits.

Fasting increases your spiritual capacity.

Fasting does not change God; it changes us, and it transforms our prayers. We don't realize the power that flows through fasting.

Hearing from God

First, fasting allows us to receive guidance, wisdom, instruction, and knowledge from God. When Moses went up on Mount Sinai, he was seeking God's will for the Israelite people, and God took him on a forty-day fast. At the end of this fast, God gave him a powerful revelation—the Law, with its Ten Commandments—which many nations have used as the foundation of their societies. All of our penal codes are based on the Law that Moses received during his forty-day fast. That's how powerful that fast was. When you fast, God is going to speak to you. You are going to receive a revelation from Him that you couldn't receive otherwise.

When you are fasting, the time you would have spent on meals should be spent in prayer and Bible study, so that you can hear what God wants to say to you. It's amazing how many hours a day are normally spent on food. Planning meals, shopping, cooking, eating, and cleaning up are very time-consuming. When you fast, all that time becomes available for you to seek God. God has always desired a close relationship with you. During a fast, there is time for true intimacy to begin to develop.

Power from God

Second, fasting enables us to receive the fullness of God's power for ministry. Sometimes prayer alone is not enough to accomplish God's purposes. The Bible tells of a man whose son was demon-possessed. Jesus' disciples were trying to cast out the demon, but the demon was laughing at them. Why? They were not prepared. Then Jesus came and cast out the demon. The disciples pulled Jesus aside and asked why they hadn't been able to do this. His answer was, *"This kind come out but only by prayer and fasting"* (Matt. 17:21 NKJV).

Christ was able to cast out any demon He was confronted with because He had spent forty days preparing Himself for ministry through prayer and fasting, and because He continued to pray and fast on a regular basis. Have you ever gone to a worship service and not felt like worshipping God? Have you ever told God you wanted to feel more of His power? It may be because you have been feeding your flesh but neglecting your spirit. Again, even though God created our physical bodies to need food, He wants them to be controlled by our spirits. I teach the Word of God almost every day of my life. I don't eat much beforehand because the worst thing to do before you speak the Word is to eat. Your flesh will get in the way of the flow of the anointing.

This is what Jesus was referring to when He told His disciples that the demon who was afflicting the man's son could come out only by prayer and fasting. He was saying, in effect, "You have prayed for this man's son to be delivered, and prayer is good. However, sometimes you need to add something to your prayers: a spirit of consecration to God and an abstinence from what can interfere with the flow of God's power in your life."

Have you ever thought, "I've been a believer for ten years, but God seems so far away. I feel so empty. I feel like I'm in the desert. I don't have any spiritual zeal. I don't have any spiritual passion for God"? Let me ask you these questions: Are you still saved? Yes. Do you still have the Holy Spirit? Yes. Then why do you feel so empty and dry? Why don't you want to go to church, read the Bible, pray, or talk to anyone about God?

To answer these questions, let's look at the example of Christ. When He was on earth, He had the full capacity of God's anointing to meet the needs of the people. Yet fasting was a necessity for Him. The Bible says, *"Jesus, **full of the Holy Spirit,** returned from the Jordan and was led by the Spirit in the desert, where for forty days he was tempted by the devil. He ate nothing during those days"* (Luke 4:1–2, emphasis added). Then it says, *"When the devil had finished all this tempting, he left him until an opportune time. Jesus returned to Galilee **in the power of the Spirit**"* (Luke 4:13–14, emphasis added).

Forty days earlier, when Jesus had been baptized by John in the Jordan, the heavens had opened and the Holy Spirit had come upon Him (Luke 3:21–22). Yet we read that, after He fasted, He returned *"in the power of the Spirit"*—whom He had already received before the fast. Jesus didn't receive the Holy Spirit after He fasted, but the Spirit within Him was manifested with new power after His fast. In John 3:34, John the Baptist said about Jesus, *"The one whom God has sent speaks the words of God, for God gives the Spirit without limit [*"measure"* NKJV]."* I believe that during Jesus' fast, God gave Him the Spirit without measure.

A fast will ignite the power of the Spirit within you.

Similarly, although you received the Holy Spirit when you were born again, a fast will ignite His power within you. When you fast, you will develop a hunger for God as well as an intimacy with Him, and the work of the Holy Spirit will be powerfully manifested in your life. Your love for the Father will be renewed. It will be a joy for you to witness to others about God's love and grace. You will be able to serve God in ways you never expected.

One of the first things Jesus encountered after His fast was a demon-possessed man. When you fast, God will send you some difficult problems because you will be ready to handle them now through His Spirit. There are people whom God wants you to minister to, but they have not yet crossed your path because you are not yet equipped to help them. Fasting will prepare you for ministry.

Breakthroughs in Difficult Situations

Third, fasting often brings breakthroughs in difficult circumstances or in the lives of those who are resistant to the Gospel. In the first chapter of Joel, we read,

> *The vine is dried up and the fig tree is withered; the pomegranate, the palm and the apple tree—all the trees of the field—are dried up. Surely the joy of mankind is withered away. Put on sackcloth, O priests,*

and mourn; wail, you who minister before the altar.
Come, spend the night in sackcloth, you who minister
before my God; for the grain offerings and drink of-
ferings are withheld from the house of your God. De-
clare a holy fast; call a sacred assembly. Summon
the elders and all who live in the land to the house of
the LORD your God, and cry out to the LORD.

(Joel 1:12–14)

This seems like a very depressing passage of Scripture, doesn't it? It talks about all the things that are lacking. Everything had gone wrong and nothing was working for the Israelites. However, the Lord had the answer. He said, *"Declare a holy fast."* Likewise, when things are tough, when you aren't experiencing a breakthrough, or nothing seems to be happening in your life, God says, "Stop everything and consecrate yourself. Come to Me." Joel 2:12–13 tells us the result of going to God:

"Even now," declares the LORD, "return to me with all
your heart, with fasting and weeping and mourning."
Rend your heart and not your garments. Return to the
LORD your God, for he is gracious and compassionate,
slow to anger and abounding in love, and he relents
from sending calamity.

In Joel 2:18–32, God said, in essence, "After you fast, get ready, because something good is going to happen. Start making some noise, because I'm getting ready to break forth." Let's look at a portion of that passage:

Be not afraid, O land; be glad and rejoice. Surely the
LORD has done great things. Be not afraid, O wild
animals, for the open pastures are becoming green.
The trees are bearing their fruit; the fig tree and the
vine yield their riches. Be glad, O people of Zion, re-
joice in the LORD your God, for he has given you the
autumn rains in righteousness. He sends you abun-
dant showers, both autumn and spring rains, as be-
fore. The threshing floors will be filled with grain; the
vats will overflow with new wine and oil. I will repay
you for the years the locusts have eaten—the great

locust and the young locust, the other locusts and the locust swarm—my great army that I sent among you.
(Joel 2:21–25)

This is the same chapter in which God prophesied about pouring out His Spirit in the last days:

Afterward, I will pour out my Spirit on all people. Your sons and daughters will prophesy, your old men will dream dreams, your young men will see visions. Even on my servants, both men and women, I will pour out my Spirit in those days. (vv. 28–29; see Acts 2:16–18)

The result of sincere fasting and prayer is that God responds, bringing deliverance and blessing.

Have you been praying and believing God about some things for a long time? You probably need to add fasting to your prayers. I used to wonder why my mother would say to my brothers and sisters and me, "All of you are going to get saved. I'm fasting for you all." My mother would often go on fasts. She would say about one of her sons, "He's running off and getting into trouble. I have to go on a fast." She used to call it "paying the price for him." Today, every one of her eleven children is born again. She saw all of them saved before she went to be with the Lord. Praying isn't enough for some children. They're so tough that you have to go a little deeper through fasting in order for them to be delivered.

Perhaps you have been trusting for years for God to bring certain family members, friends, and acquaintances to Christ. It is possible that the evil spirits from the enemy who are deceiving them aren't going to leave unless you add fasting to your prayers. Or perhaps you have been praying for a breakthrough at your workplace. You can fast for that situation, also. You can say to God, "Father, I'm consecrating myself. I'm setting myself apart for this situation at work." When you "pay the price" by praying and fasting, God will respond.

Praying isn't always enough. Sometimes only prayer *and* fasting can bring deliverance.

THE RIGHT WAY TO FAST

When we consecrate ourselves, we need to be careful not to hinder the effectiveness of our fasting. It must be done in the right spirit. Isaiah 58 tells us right and wrong ways to fast. In verse three, God quoted the Israelites: *"'Why have we fasted,' they say, 'and you have not seen it? Why have we humbled ourselves, and you have not noticed?'"* His reply was,

> *Yet on the day of your fasting, you do as you please and exploit all your workers. Your fasting ends in quarreling and strife, and in striking each other with wicked fists. You cannot fast as you do today and expect your voice to be heard on high.* (vv. 3–4)

What was the problem with the Israelites' fasting? It was characterized by injustice to others and ended in *"quarreling and strife."* I imagine they were saying things like, "Did you notice that So-and-So broke his fast?" or "I fast more than you do." They were in competition with one another—even in spiritual matters. That's striving.

When God says, *"Declare a holy fast; call a sacred assembly"* (Joel 1:14), He is saying, "Call people away from their regular duties and have them fast as a holy duty to Me." If anyone wants to get serious with God, he must show it by his commitment to doing the things he should be doing—with the right attitude. If we "do as we please" when we fast, instead of seeking and obeying God, He will say to us, "Do you expect Me to answer your prayers while you have this attitude?

This is no game. Either you're fasting, or you're on some kind of diet. If you're on a diet, you can watch television, play computer games, or do whatever you want. However, if you're going to consecrate yourself before Me, then you have to set yourself apart and seek Me rather than your own interests." That is what we have to do if we want God to be pleased with our fasts. God wants us to earnestly seek Him and His ways. In turn, He will pour out His power through us.

Is not this the kind of fasting I have chosen: to loose the chains of injustice and untie the cords of the yoke, to set the oppressed free and break every yoke? Is it not to share your food with the hungry and to provide the poor wanderer with shelter—when you see the naked, to clothe him, and not to turn away from your own flesh and blood? Then your light will break forth like the dawn, and your healing will quickly appear; then your righteousness will go before you, and the glory of the LORD will be your rear guard. Then you will call, and the LORD will answer; you will cry for help, and he will say: Here am I....The LORD will guide you always; he will satisfy your needs in a sun-scorched land and will strengthen your frame. You will be like a well-watered garden, like a spring whose waters never fail. (Isa. 58:6–9, 11)

Isaiah says that the fast God is pleased with has the power to break the chains of injustice and destroy the yokes of the oppressed. God's anointing can deliver people from their burdens. This anointing comes through fasting that is consecrated and committed to God. Therefore, a true fast will cause you to understand and value the important things in life. You will become a giver. You will begin to love people and want to meet their needs. You will have a burden for souls.

Isaiah 58:12 tells us the outcome of such a fast: *"Your people will rebuild the ancient ruins and will raise up the age-old foundations; you will be called Repairer of Broken Walls, Restorer of Streets with Dwellings."* People's lives will be restored to God, and you will also receive God's blessings. For example, verse eight says, *"Then your light will break forth like the dawn, and your healing will quickly appear."* You have an opportunity to activate your faith for healing when you fast. Perhaps you've been praying for healing for a long time. God is saying, "Because you are willing to consecrate yourself to Me

Fasting will cause people's lives to be restored—and you also will receive God's blessings.

and humble yourself on behalf of others, I'm going to bring healing speedily."

Isaiah 58:8 also says, *"Your righteousness will go before you, and the glory of the LORD will be your rear guard."* The Lord will protect you. If people set traps for you, God will say, in effect, "That is one of My consecrated saints; don't touch him." These and other blessings will come as a result of a fast that is pleasing to God.

READY TO BE FILLED

Are you tired of praying, and having no results? When you fast, you're setting yourself up for answered prayer. God has promised that if you fast in the right way, He will hear and answer. *"Then you will call, and the LORD will answer; you will cry for help, and he will say: Here am I"* (Isa. 58:9). Why will God answer your prayers? It is because, when you fast, you are open to Him. Your spiritual capacity to hear and receive is increased. You are empty of your own interests, and you are ready for Him to fill you.

LET'S PRAY TOGETHER

Heavenly Father,

You have taught us that when we pray, we are to bring others' needs with us. Fasting is a form of intercession, and we want to be empowered by Your Spirit through fasting so we can minister to others and counteract the work of the enemy. We consecrate ourselves to You in prayer and fasting, setting ourselves apart to seek You and Your will, rather than our own interests. Use us to fulfill Your purposes for Your glory. We pray this in the name of Jesus, who fasted and prayed not only for His disciples, but also for us who have believed in Him through their testimony (John 17:20). Amen.

PUTTING PRAYER INTO PRACTICE

Ask yourself:

- Do my prayers tend to focus on myself or on others?
- Is there a situation in my life, or a person for whom I am praying, that is resistant to prayer?
- Do I hear from God and experience the power of His Spirit to meet the needs of myself and others?
- Is fasting a regular practice in my life?

Action Steps:

- Compare Isaiah 58:6–9 with 1 John 3:14–19 and Matthew 25:31–40. In what ways do the New Testament passages reinforce what God said is important to Him during a fast, which He described in the passage from Isaiah?
- Considering the kind of fast that pleases God, what is one way you can help meet someone's spiritual or physical needs this week?
- Set aside a time to consecrate yourself in prayer and fasting on behalf of someone else who needs a breakthrough.

Principles

1. God expects His people to fast; it is not an option. In the same way we practice the habits of Bible reading and prayer, we should also practice the habit of fasting.
2. A fast is a conscious, intentional decision to abstain for a time from the pleasure of eating in order to gain spiritual benefits.
3. The following are characteristics of fasting:
   - Fasting is a time set apart to seek the face of God and to abstain from other things in order to give one's whole heart to God in prayer.
   - Fasting means putting God first, focusing all of one's attention on Him alone.
   - Fasting is a time to foster a sensitive environment for the working of prayer.
   - Fasting is a form of intercession for others.
4. Fasting does not change God; it changes us and our prayers.
5. The results of fasting are:
   - *Hearing from God:* Fasting allows us to receive guidance, wisdom, instruction, and knowledge from God.
   - *Power from God:* Fasting enables us to receive the fullness of the Spirit for ministry.
   - *Breakthroughs in Difficult Situations:* Fasting brings breakthroughs in difficult circumstances and in the lives of those who are resistant to the Gospel.
6. According to Isaiah 58, right and wrong ways to fast are:
   - *Right:* Being consecrated and committed to God, fasting while having the right priorities, lifting people's burdens, having the heart of a giver, showing love to others, and having a burden for souls.
   - *Wrong:* Fasting while treating others with injustice, quarreling and striving; pursuing our own pleasures rather than God's will.
7. The outcomes of a true fast are the following:
   - People are delivered and restored to God.
   - The one who fasts receives God's blessings.

Conclusion:
Becoming a Person of Prayer

Your kingdom come. Your will be done on earth as it is in heaven.
—Matthew 6:10 (NKJV)

Prayer is not an option. It is a necessity!

In this book, we have explored many powerful principles in regard to prayer. Prayer is our invitation to God to intervene in the affairs of earth, our agreement with His sovereign will, our request for Him to work His ways in this world. It is a vital part of God's purpose in creation—and it is something we are called to pursue.

I would like to challenge you to take the principles of this book and test them. Begin praying according to the Word of God and in the name of Jesus. Review the thought questions and action steps at the end of each chapter and put them into practice. Discover your power, your authority, and your rights as an intercessor for the earth.

In short, become a person of prayer.

A PERSON OF PRAYER

A person of prayer—

- Knows that prayer is a sacred trust from God.
- Understands his or her purpose in life as God's priest and intercessor for the world.
- Has a relationship of trust with the heavenly Father and desires the world to experience the power of His presence and life.
- Knows that the will of God will flow forth from heaven to earth only through his prayers and the prayers of all God's people.

Conclusion: Becoming a Person of Prayer

If we know God's plan for prayer, yet fail to pursue it, we are like a person who sees his reflection in the mirror, but then immediately forgets what he looks like. (See James 1:22–25.) The absolute necessity of prayer must be like an indelible image upon our hearts and minds. If we want to see God's will done on earth, we must do our part—we must *pray*.

God desires you to partner with Him in the great purpose of reclaiming and redeeming the world. The Scripture says, *"If my people, who are called by my name, will humble themselves and pray and seek my face and turn from their wicked ways, then will I hear from heaven and will forgive their sin and will heal their land"* (2 Chron. 7:14). God is saying, *"If my people,...then will I."* Once again, God has called His people to be His priests or intercessors—this refers to the *entire* body of Christ, not just an elite group of "Intercessory Prayer Warriors" in the local church. All of us have the power to bring God's will on earth so the world can be healed and transformed by His grace.

Remember, what happens on earth is not determined by God but is determined by what He allows. God's will can be executed only through the cooperation of mankind on earth. Prayer is this medium of cooperation. Prayer is therefore the most important activity of humanity.

Use the purpose and position God has given you to invite heaven to intervene in the realm of earth. Prepare your heart, mind, soul, and strength to wholly agree that God's will be done on earth until *"the kingdom of the world has become the kingdom of our Lord and of his Christ"* (Rev. 11:15).

The earth is depending on you to pray. The families of the earth are depending on you to pray. Your children's children are depending on you to pray. All creation is depending on you to pray. Heaven is depending on you to pray. I challenge you:

Fulfill your obligation to your generation and to the future of planet earth.

About the Author

D
r. Myles Munroe is an international motivational speaker, best-selling author, lecturer, educator, and consultant for government and business. Traveling extensively throughout the world, Dr. Munroe addresses critical issues affecting the full range of human, social, and spiritual development. The central theme of his message is the transformation of followers into leaders and the maximization of individual potential.

Dr. Munroe is founder and president of Bahamas Faith Ministries International (BFMI), an all-encompassing network of ministries headquartered in Nassau, Bahamas. He is president and chief executive officer of the International Third World Leaders Association and the International Third World Leadership Training Institute. Dr. Munroe is also the founder, executive producer, and principal host of a number of radio, television, and global network programs aired worldwide. He is a contributing writer for numerous Bible editions, magazines, and newsletters, including *The Believer's Topical Bible, The African Cultural Heritage Topical Bible, Charisma Life Christian Magazine,* and *Ministries Today.* He has earned degrees from Oral Roberts University and the University of Tulsa, and he was awarded an honorary doctorate from Oral Roberts University, where he is an adjunct professor in the Graduate School of Theology.

Dr. Munroe and his wife, Ruth, travel as a team, teaching and ministering with sensitive hearts. They are the proud parents of two young adults, Charisa and Myles, Jr.

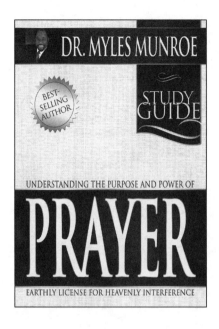

Understanding the Purpose and Power of Prayer
Study Guide
Dr. Myles Munroe

Designed for either individual or small group study, this companion guide to *Understanding the Purpose and Power of Prayer* will ignite and transform the way you pray! Dr. Myles Munroe's biblically-based, time-tested prayer principles will take the mystery out of communicating with God. In these pages, you'll explore deeper insights and thought-provoking questions for life application of these powerful truths. Discover a new dimension of faith, a deeper revelation of God's love, and a renewed understanding that you can pray—and receive results.

ISBN: 978-0-88368-890-8 • Workbook • 144 pages

WHITAKER
HOUSE

www.whitakerhouse.com

The Most Important Person on Earth:
The Holy Spirit, Governor of the Kingdom

Dr. Myles Munroe

In *The Most Important Person on Earth*, Dr. Myles Munroe explains
how the Holy Spirit is the Governor of God's kingdom on earth,
much as royal governors administered the will of earthly kings
in their territories. Under the guidance and enabling of the Holy
Spirit, you will discover how to bring order to the chaos in your life,
receive God's power to heal and deliver, fulfill your true purpose
with joy, become a leader in your sphere of influence, and be part of
God's government on earth. Enter into the fullness of God's Spirit
as you embrace God's design for your life today.

ISBN: 978-0-88368-986-8 • Hardcover • 320 pages

www.whitakerhouse.com